Beste İşleyen

# The European Union
# in the Middle East Peace Process

# A Civilian Power?

AN INTERDISCIPLINARY SERIES
OF THE CENTRE FOR INTERCULTURAL AND EUROPEAN STUDIES

INTERDISZIPLINÄRE SCHRIFTENREIHE
DES CENTRUMS FÜR INTERKULTURELLE UND EUROPÄISCHE STUDIEN

CINTEUS · Fulda University of Applied Sciences · Hochschule Fulda

ISSN 1865-2255

4    *Stamatia Devetzi und Hans-Wolfgang Platzer (Hrsg.)*
     Offene Methode der Koordinierung und Europäisches Sozialmodell
     Interdisziplinäre Perspektiven
     ISBN 978-3-89821-994-5

5    *Andrea Rudolf*
     Biokraftstoffpolitik und Ernährungssicherheit
     Die Auswirkungen der EU-Politik auf die Nahrungsmittelproduktion am
     Beispiel Brasilien
     ISBN 978-3-8382-0099-6

6    *Gudrun Hentges / Justyna Staszczak*
     Geduldet, nicht erwünscht
     Auswirkungen der Bleiberechtsregelung auf die Lebenssituation geduldeter
     Flüchtlinge in Deutschland
     ISBN 978-3-8382-0080-4

7    *Barbara Lewandowska-Tomaszczyk / Hanna Pułaczewska (Eds. / Hrsg.)*
     Intercultural Europe
     Arenas of Difference, Communication and Mediation
     ISBN 978-3-8382-0198-6

**Series Editors**

Gudrun Hentges
Volker Hinnenkamp
Anne Honer
Hans-Wolfgang Platzer

Fachbereich Sozial- und Kulturwissenschaften
Hochschule Fulda University of Applied Sciences
Marquardstraße 35
D-36039 Fulda

cinteus@sk.hs-fulda.de
www.cinteus.eu

Beste İşleyen

# THE EUROPEAN UNION
# IN THE MIDDLE EAST PEACE PROCESS

## A Civilian Power?

*ibidem*-Verlag
Stuttgart

**Bibliografische Information der Deutschen Nationalbibliothek**
Die Deutsche Nationalbibliothek verzeichnet diese Publikation in der
Deutschen Nationalbibliografie; detaillierte bibliografische Daten sind im
Internet über http://dnb.d-nb.de abrufbar.

**Bibliographic information published by the Deutsche Nationalbibliothek**
Die Deutsche Nationalbibliothek lists this publication in the Deutsche Nationalbibliografie;
detailed bibliographic data are available in the Internet at http://dnb.d-nb.de.

∞

Gedruckt auf alterungsbeständigem, säurefreien Papier
Printed on acid-free paper

ISSN: 1865-2255

ISBN-10: 3-89821-896-1
ISBN-13: 978-3-89821-896-2

Zweite, bearbeitete und ergänzte Auflage

© *ibidem*-Verlag
Stuttgart 2011

Alle Rechte vorbehalten

Printed in Germany

## Editorial

This series is intended as a publication panel of the Centre of Intercultural and European Studies (CINTEUS) at Fulda University of Applied Sciences. The series aims at making research results, anthologies, conference readers, study books and selected qualification theses accessible to the general public. It comprises of scientific and interdisciplinary works on inter- and transculturality; the European Union from an interior and a global perspective; and problems of social welfare and social law in Europe. Each of these are fields of research and teaching in the Social- and Cultural Studies Faculty at Fulda University of Applied Sciences and its Centre for Intercultural and European Studies. We also invite contributions from outside the faculty that share and enrich our research.

Gudrun Hentges, Volker Hinnenkamp, Anne Honer & Hans-Wolfgang Platzer

## Editorial

Die Buchreihe versteht sich als Publikationsforum des Centrums für interkulturelle und europäische Studien (CINTEUS) der Hochschule Fulda. Ziel der CINTEUS-Reihe ist es, Forschungsergebnisse, Anthologien, Kongressreader, Studienbücher und ausgewählte Qualifikationsarbeiten einer interessierten Öffentlichkeit zugänglich zu machen. Die Reihe umfasst fachwissenschaftliche und interdisziplinäre Arbeiten aus den Bereichen Inter- und Transkulturalität, Europäische Union aus Binnen- und globaler Perspektive sowie wohlfahrtsstaatliche und sozialrechtliche Probleme Europas. All dies sind Fachgebiete, die im Fachbereich Sozial- und Kulturwissenschaften der Hochschule Fulda University of Applied Sciences und dem angegliederten Centrum für interkulturelle und Europastudien gelehrt und erforscht werden. Ausdrücklich eingeladen an der Publikationsreihe mitzuwirken sind auch solche Studien, die nicht 'im Hause' entstanden sind, aber CINTEUS-Schwerpunkte berühren und bereichern.

Gudrun Hentges, Volker Hinnenkamp, Anne Honer & Hans-Wolfgang Platzer

## Foreword to "The European Union in the Middle East Peace Process: A Civilian Power?"

The European Union's role in international relations and its foreign and security policies have been the subject of comprehensive and continuously growing research. The same applies to the academic discussion of the Israel-Palestine conflict and the peace process in the Middle East.

İşleyen's study provides an important and enriching contribution to these debates; it is able to appeal to a broad audience, above all due to its specific theoretical conception and the focus of its contents.

At the theoretical level this study takes up the political debate on the concept of "civilian power" and argues, by critically discussing the pertinent schools of thought, that and how the "concept of civilian power" is appropriate to encompass attributes for self-description used by the EU as well as characteristics of the EU's international-policy practice.

Since the – initially modest – beginnings of a common EU foreign policy in the 1970s it has been accompanied by conflicts over its preconditions, quality and scope. "Symbolism" and "substance" were central concepts of this controversy for a long time.

At present the debate pivots around the particular actor role of the EU as an internally differentiated community strongly intertwined with the exterior world. Numerous observers see the EU as the normative model for empirical practice realising a civilian power which follows the primacy of diplomacy und structured international dialogues, which prefers economic interdependence and incentives, and promotes the multi-lateral implementation of rules for the challenges of security and environmental policies. Compared to the super power or the neutral community this international role is even often seen as the more modern answer to the current challenges of an interdependent, globalised world. Recently more and more voices are arising, however, that consider the military and defence policy efforts of the EU as a threat and a challenge to this very character of a civilian power.

This book processes this debate concisely and thus gains an analytical set of instruments that are applied to the Middle East policy of the EU and the EU's contribution to a solution of the Israel-Palestine conflict. The brief historical reconstruction of the EU's role in this conflict and the differentiated discussion of its instruments of action shows an EU between "payer and player". The analysis identifies the specific characteristics and the action potential of the EU but also its limits as a civilian power, which are not least due to the internal preconditions and institutional mechanisms of this novel alliance of states.

Hans-Wolfgang Platzer

## Acknowledgements

I feel obliged to especially thank my supervisor and intellectual guide, Prof. Dr. Hans-Wolfgang Platzer, at the Department of Social and Cultural Studies at the Fulda University of Applied Sciences, for his personal contributions and helpful suggestions. I would also like to thank Prof. Dr. Erich Ott, who gave invaluable insights and comments at various stages.

Special thanks belong to Prof. Dr. Volker Hinnenkamp, who insisted it should be published, and to the *ibidem* publishing company. Thanks also belong to the library of the German Council on Foreign Relations (DGAP) in Berlin for the use of their collections. I am also grateful to my family and friends who encouraged me to publish it.

November 2007                                                    Beste İşleyen

## Contents

# 1. Introduction

The Middle East[1] and particularly the Arab-Israeli conflict[2] have occupied a high-ranking position on the agenda of the European Union (EU), whose primary objective is to ensure the economic and political stability in its southeastern neighbourhood. Since the unanimous adoption of the Schuman Declaration in 1971, the EU has continuously declared its position towards the unsettled issues, including the occupied territories and the status of Jerusalem, and sought, at the same time, a stronger political role in international peace initiatives.

Indeed, the rhetoric of EU representatives and official EU Declarations on the situation in the Middle East contain explicit references to the Union's "willingness" to work in close cooperation with regional and international actors towards a long lasting peace settlement. Meanwhile, there have been intensive efforts at the EU level to move towards common positions and set up a more coherent Middle East Policy that would be consistent with the Community's economic and political interests in the region. Nevertheless, though it has developed remarkably over the years, the EU involvement in the Middle East peace process (MEPP) has been, to some extent, limited to an economic engagement, rather than a political role.

The aim of this study is to examine the EU's policy towards the Middle East, since its launch in the 1970s, and to illustrate and analyse the internal factors that constitute an obstacle to the enhancement of the European political presence in the region.

---

[1] In this study, the term Middle East comprises Egypt, Jordan, Lebanon, Syria, Israel, and the West Bank and Gaza Strip.

[2] The Arab-Israeli conflict refers to the political disputes and open hostilities between the Arab countries of the Middle East and Israel, which emerged after the establishment of the State of Israel in 1948 with the UN Partition Plan of 1947, and remains unsolved ever since (Süer et al. 2006). The Arab-Israeli conflict is also called the Middle East conflict. However, in this study, the main focus will be given to the Israeli-Palestinian conflict, which is a still ongoing confrontation between the Arab Palestinians and the Jewish Israelis, who both claim the right over the Land of Palestine/Israel.

In the first part (chapter 2), before assessing the historical evolution of the EU Middle East Policy, the "civilian power concept" will be thoroughly examined with a comprehensive analysis of the past and current debates over the topic. The next step will be to apply the notion of civilian power to the European case, and to find out whether the EU can be identified as a civilian power. After this introduction, the root causes of civilian power Europe (CPE) are discussed with a major focus on an approach that focuses on the internal dynamics of EU foreign policy formulation. A brief historical summary of the developments in European foreign policy cooperation - from the European Political Cooperation (EPC) to the Common Foreign and Security Policy (CFSP) - together with a review of the institutional constraints and the decision-making mechanism in EU foreign policy pillar will serve to better understand whether and if so, why the EU operates as a civilian power.

The third chapter will scrutinise the historical development of European policy towards the Arab-Israeli conflict from the first initiatives in the 1970s to the Roadmap of 2003. It examines the past and present positions of the EU in the peace process, which are consistent with the institutional developments in the EU foreign policy arena. The division of the third chapter into two main categories is mainly due to the commonly shared view among the scholars that it was with the incorporation of the CFSP into one institutional framework and the expansion of the scope of decision-making that the EU started to act collectively and speak with a single voice in its relations with other parties. Here, a chronological analysis of the EU involvement in the region will help to better comprehend how the EU has developed its policy toward the region, and gradually developed its position to an influential partner in the MEPP. Furthermore, this chapter demonstrates the economic and diplomatic achievements of the EU as well as the weaknesses, particularly within the framework of foreign policy cooperation among the member states.

In the fifth and the sixth chapters, in order to demonstrate the importance of the EU involvement in the peace process as well as the (in)effectiveness of its policies towards the conflicting parties, the EU relations with the Palestinian Authority and Israel, in both economic and political terms, will be analysed in detail. The part dealing with the EU-Palestinian relations pays primary attention to the EU financial assistance to the state- and institution-building in the occupied territories and to several other development projects. The second part outlines the EU's bilateral and multilateral relations with Israel. This section also focuses on the areas where the EU has succeeded in speaking with a single voice, and where it has failed to do so.

Finally, by comparing the main features of an ideal civilian power with the EU policy towards the Arab-Israeli conflict, the last chapter will examine whether the EU, with its role in the Middle East peace process, can be defined as a civilian power. This part also studies the root causes of this kind of foreign policy conduct.

## 2. Theoretical framework

The European Union, considered to be *sui generis,* is an extremely complex organisation combining both supranational and intergovernmental elements in its unique system of governance (Peterson et al. 1999, 5). Owing to this multi-level structure within the EU and the complexity of the decision-making mechanism in different stages of policy-making, no single traditional theory of International Relations (IR) can explain the entire range of EU foreign policy conduct and the gradual evolution of its position towards the Middle East conflict. This is summed up in the words of Greilsammer et al., who state that the "examination of European policy towards the Israeli-Palestinian conflict takes us in several senses to the limits, or even beyond, classical models of foreign policy analysis" (Greilsammer et al. 1984, 121).

The "civilian power" concept is one possible theoretical approach to the examination of the historical development of a European position towards the Arab-Israeli conflict as well as the operation of a common European strategy towards the Middle East peace process within the framework of both the EPC and the CFSP.

The following section of the study examines the concept of civilian power, as well as contentious issues such as the nature of an ideal civilian power, its foreign policy conduct and the use of force by civilian powers. A detailed analysis of how the conception of civilian power has been used and developed over the years will serve to better understand whether the idea is applicable to the European case.

### 2.1. Civilian power concept

One of the well-known conceptual categorizations used to characterise and examine the international role of the EC/EU is the idea of "civilian power Europe", which was first applied to the EC by François Duchêne. Despite the lack of an explicit definition of either the nature or the foreign policy conduct of a civilian power, Duchêne's notion of civilian power Europe has occupied a notable position in academic debates over the international role of the EC/EU

(Smith 2000; Bretherton et al. 2006). Duchêne defined the Community as follows:

> "The EC will only make the most of its opportunities if it remains true to its inner characteristics. They are primarily: civilian ends and means and a built-in sense of collective action, which in turn express, however imperfectly, social values of equality, justice and tolerance" (Duchêne 1973, 20).

Duchêne assumed that the Community, consisting of a "civilian group of countries long on economic power and relatively short on armed force", has an interest in domesticating its "relations between States including those of its own members and those with States outside its frontiers." Defining the European Community as "an exemplar of a new stage in political civilisation", Duchêne argued that domestication of Community's international relations would mean "to bring to international problems the common sense of responsibility and structures of contractual politics which have in past been associated almost exclusively with "home" and not foreign, that is, *alien* affairs" (Duchêne 1973, 19-20).

However, Duchêne's idea of civilian power Europe has not been without its critics. [3] During the Cold War, Hedley Bull argued that civilian power Europe is a "contradiction in terms" and pointed to the Community's lack of military capabilities. Bull challenged the argument made by the proponents of the civilian power concept that the increase in the importance of questions regarding social, political and cultural matters in the 1960s had proven the irrelevance of military strength and power politics in international affairs. The essence of Bull's criticism was that at that time, "the power or influence exerted by the European Community and other such civilian actors was conditional upon a strategic environment provided by the military power of states, which they did not control." Therefore, civilian power Europe was mainly due to "the vulnerability of the countries in Western Europe." Lastly, Bull urged Western Europe to acquire military capabilities since strategic issues still maintained their significance, (Bull 1982, 151). Despite this criticism, CPE is still a topic of intense research and debate in academic circles. Although "Duchêne never

---

[3] See Bretherton et al. (2006) and Foradori (2006).

developed his vision into a detailed and comprehensive scheme" (Zielonka quoted in Orbie 2006, 123) the literature on EU external affairs offers numerous studies with references to Duchêne's 1973 article.

Duchêne's idea of the EU as a civilian power was developed by Hanns Maull, whose ideas were primarily articulated to analyse the foreign policy behaviour of Germany and Japan after the Second World War. Maull identified the implications of a civilian power as follows:

"a) the acceptance of the necessity of cooperation with others in the pursuit of international objectives;

b) the concentration on non-military, primarily economic, means to secure national goals, with military power left as a residual instrument serving essentially to safeguard other means of international interaction; and

c) a willingness to develop supranational structures to address critical issues of international management" (Maull 1990, 92-93).

Maull assumed that international order can be established and fostered with the existence of civilian powers, defined as states dependent on economic co-operation, supranational bodies and principally economic (and non-military) means. Maull argued that as a result of important changes in interstate relations, a new understanding of international affairs flourished which significantly differed from traditional interstate relations relying on security considerations and changes caused by wars. In contemporary world politics, civilian powers might play an important role. Maull asserted that civilian powers display industrial strength, for which they depend on international economic co-operation, and a clear weakness in military might. However, Maull's arguments were based almost exclusively on rationalist cost-and-benefit calculations, such as economic and foreign policy consequences rather than values and principles. His characterisation of civilian power is incomplete in the sense that it puts its primary emphasis on the "means" applied by civilian powers, namely; economic and non-military, and omits to specify what kind of "ends" they pursue. Except for mentioning that "the development of the rule of the law in international relations (...) helps to push forward the process of "civilising" [4], international politics, Maull's definition lacks a clear identification of what a civilian power seeks to achieve in foreign policy. Yet, Maull pointed that "solidarity with other societies, and a sense of responsibility for the future of the world – and particularly the global environment – are values that will have to be inculcated" (Maull 1990, 106). Moreover, according to Maull's definition, military might, though seen as a final tool, is not totally repudiated if it serves "essentially to safeguard other means of international interaction."[5]

Later in a research project funded by the German Research Association, Maull, with four other scholars, developed the notion of civilian power as a new method for international relations analysis. A comparative study of the foreign policy approaches of Germany, Japan and the United States (U.S.), the research project was conducted with the intention of revealing to what extent the foreign policy behaviour of the above mentioned countries resemble to that of a civilian power. Based on role theory[6], the study makes the argument that with time, states construct particular and diversified patterns of national role-conceptions which, accompanied by external role-conceptions, constitute their foreign policy identity. Internal factors constructing a state's external identity encompass a society's cognitive system, public opinion and various other political elements such as political parties and interest groups. External factors, on the other hand, include historical experiences and inter-

---

[4] Elias (1976) argued that over the past centuries, Western Europe countries have showed an ever growing rejection of the use of force and sought to "civilize" societal relations. For Elias, physical violence has become an irrelevant instrument in those societies and Western countries have gradually adopted various norms and values that started to determine social practices. With time, normative principles have become more and more inherent in political relations. Maull (1999) argues that Elias' argument has important implications for international relations, since there is an interplay between "civilized" domestic politics and foreign policy behaviour. Furthermore, with the help of a "civilization hexagon", Dieter Senghaas (1994, 26) defines the main goals in the "civilizing" process. Accordingly, Senghaas regards "peace as a civilization process" (11, my translation), which includes a wide range of elements such as the non-use of violence, the rule of law, democratic participation, interdependence and institutionalized conflict settlement and social equality. Though Senghaas puts forward these elements to examine domestic politics, he argues that they can, though not entirely in content and form, be transferred to international arena.

[5] There is an academic debate in the literature over the question whether a civilian power can use force. See part 2.3. of this study.

[6] See chapter 2.4.2.2. of this study for a brief analysis of role-theory.

national socialization. Therefore, identification of each state's role-conception is considered to contribute to elucidate and, to a lesser degree, even predict their foreign policy behaviour.

In this context, civilian power is regarded as a specific foreign policy role-conception, whose identity implies the following roles: a) an initiator/promoter of international action aiming to civilise international relations; b) a welfare maximizer interested in democratic stability and social justice; c) a suprana-tionalist willing to transfer sovereignty by strengthening international institu-tions; a regime builder/deepener/enlarger, and promoter of the rule of law, in-ternational institutions and regimes; d) a propagator of interdependent inter-ests and promoter of universal values such as democracy, human rights and good governance; e) a collective actor and an opponent of unilateral action with a foreign policy style based on collective action, compromise and nego-tiation; and lastly f) a promoter of collective and cooperative security and supporter of multilateral instruments (Maull et al. 1997, 26-29).

The civilian means mentioned in this study are diplomatic and political instru-ments; civilian ends on the other hand, include international cooperation, do-mestication of international relations, strengthening the rule of law and institu-tions and diffusion of universal values such as democracy, human rights, equality, and good governance. The project conducted by Maull et al. makes a significant contribution to civilian power concept, since the model presented in the study is a comprehensive analytical framework encompassing both ci-vilian means and civilian ends.

The objectives Maull et al. specify resemble Arnold Wolfers' (1962) "milieu goals" which differ from "possession goals." For Wolfers, a nation with foreign policy focussed on the attainment of possession goals, is interested princi-pally in reinforcing or defending values such as territory extension, member-ship in leading international institutions or tariff preferences. Here, the nation struggles to acquire a "share in values of limited supply." Milieu goals, how-ever, are directed to "the shape of the environment in which a nation oper-ates." As opposed to nations with possession goals, those pursuing milieu goals do not attempt to exclude other nations from the international scene by trying to preserve and increase their possessions. Instead, they seek to shape the environment outside their boundaries through the establishment of international organisations. Wolfers warned that milieu goals may be misused by some and may only serve as an instrument to gain possession goals. So, the nation expects to preserve and even increase its status and security by establishing international organisations. Yet, the nation in question might be seriously concerned with the milieu and might devote all its resources, including international organisations, to ensure a stable political order (Wolfers 1962, 73-76).

Orbie (2006) suggests that the distinctiveness of the civilian power concept lies in that the notion demonstrates the tendency in IR literature to provide alternative explanations to world affairs as well as to EC/EU external relations. For Orbie, CPE is a challenge to the realist school in the sense that the former refers to a wide range features that might shape foreign policy behavior that are not mentioned by traditional IR theories. Orbie argues that Duchêne's conceptualizations pointed to the primacy of international interdependence in economic issues. Moreover, Duchêne also referred to the possibility of developing common understandings about international affairs. For Orbie these two elements – use of economic/non-military instruments and respect of universally accepted values - make the EU a unique foreign policy actor.

Another important issue to be discussed is how a civilian power uses its means to achieve its desired ends. Smith (2005) argues that in addition to civilian objectives and tools, civilian powers also differ from traditional actors in terms of their distinctive way of behaving in their pursuit of their goals. This is related to the "how" question. Smith argues that the four categories that Christopher Hill introduces to identify the way in which civilian powers perform in the international arena refer to the third aspect of civilian powers, which is, in Smith's own words: "how an actor uses its means to try to achieve its ends" (Smith 2005, 3). Christopher Hill puts forward four ways in which an actor performs in the international arena. For Hill, an actor may either force another actor to do something by using "stick" or deterrence (the threat of using force), or it may try to exercise influence on others' decisions by using "carrot" and deference (latent influence). He differentiates the "civilian model" from the "power blocs" by pointing out that "civilian powers rely on soft power, on persuasion and attraction; not on coercion or carrots or sticks." Power blocs, on the other hand, use coercion (Hill quoted in Smith 2005, 4).

The concept of "soft power" was first introduced by Joseph Nye. As Smith rightly points out, Nye's concept of 'soft power' entails certain similarities with Hill's definition of "carrots" and "deterrence" (2005: 4). What is soft-power according to Nye? Nye defines the soft power or co-optive power as "the ability to get what you want through attraction rather than coercion or payments" (2004: X). The main component of his argument is that "hard power" (or coercive as Nye calls it), which is sharply in contrast to soft power, refers to inducements or threats, in Hill's words to "carrots and sticks." As Nye points out, hard power is not always an obligatory or advantageous strategy for accomplishing foreign policy goals, since nations are sometimes confronted with disputes that cannot be overcome solely by traditional means. In this case, as Nye assumes, soft power, which is a nation's ability to develop relations through persuasion and attraction, rather than military or financial coercion, is a more attractive and desirable method (Nye 2004, 153-170).

Furthermore, according to Nye, the extent to which the culture, values, and institutions receive admiration and respect in the milieu is also vital for the reason that "a country may obtain the outcomes it wants in world politics because other countries – admiring its values, emulating its example, aspiring to its level of prosperity and openness – want to follow it" (Nye 2004, 5). In this context, power resources involve cultural attraction, ideology, and international institutions (Nye 1990).

Similarly, Manners (2006) argues that civilian power can be identified in terms of its aims, nature and strategies. Manners puts forward four important elements to differentiate civilian powers from other conceptual categorizations applied to the EC/EU. First, a key feature of CPE is that it seeks to "civilize the world" (175). Second, Europe as a civilian power seeks economic instruments, rather than military tools, for achieving their national interests. Third, Manners argues that civilian power concept puts "emphasis on international society as the forms and means of world politics" (176). Fourth, CPE treats the EC/EU as an agent in world politics despite the fact that the central issue areas are multilateral, economic and legal rather than hard policy issue.

The elements a civilian power is expected to entail are therefore the "means" it makes use of, the "ends" it intends to achieve and the "way" those means are applied (Smith 2005). Smith (2005) adds a fourth element, namely; the "process" by which the foreign policy is performed. By creating an ideal type that she calls "albeit approximate", Smith explicitly specifies the four elements a civilian power is supposed to possess: "Civilian power is an actor which uses civilian means for persuasion, to pursue civilian ends, and whose foreign policy-making process is subject to democratic control or public scrutiny. All four elements are important" (Smith 2005, 5).

Besides, in order to make a comparison, Smith puts forward an opposite ideal type, namely; a military power. Smith assumes that though rather difficult to predict, such a military power would be an actor that uses military means and relies on coercion to exercise power over other actors, unilaterally aiming at obtaining "military or militarised ends" (here goals might include territorial conquest and more military power), and whose foreign policy is not democratic. In brief, the elements Smith puts forward to define a military and civilian power are the means, ends, the manner in which these means are used, and lastly, the process in which foreign policy is conducted (Smith 2005, 5).

In the next step, Smith creates "a spectrum of powers in international relations" with civilian and military power at either end. On this spectrum Smith tries to position nations according to their foreign policy behaviours, and comes to the conclusion that the majority of states located along the spectrum are close to one of the ideal types, yet they are not exactly at the end. Smith argues that North Korea, Hitler's Germany and Saddam's Iraq could be identified as military powers. In contrast, Europe's neutral states (Austria, Finland, Ireland, Sweden and Switzerland), regardless of their military might and involvement in UN operations, debatably come "closest" to ideal civilian powers. In this sense, "their military posture is primarily defensive (of the national territory)" (Smith 2005, 6).

In short, being a civilian power entails the application of civilian means, primarily economic instruments; the pursuit of civilian ends, such as international cooperation, solidarity, the rule of law, and the promotion of peace, democracy and justice; and the application of persuasion and negotiation methods when using civilian means. The question that remains to be answered is whether the European Union can be identified as a civilian power. To answer this question, the next section will focus on the self-characterisation and the foreign policy making of the EU.

## 2.2.    Is the EU a civilian power?

### 2.2.1.  Self-Characterisation of the EU

Smith argues that "a structural requirement for "international actor capability" is the existence of commonly accepted goals, along with a system for mobilizing resources necessary to meet the goals" (Smith 2003, 9) In the light of this explanation and following the assumptions of CPE (objectives and instruments) this part analyses EU declarations in order to demonstrate to what extent the self-conception of the EU contains elements of the civilian power model.

The self-characterisation of the European Union contains explicit elements of the civilian power model. Since its first foreign policy attempts, the EU has repeatedly expressed its self-perception, along with its responsibility towards the outer world, in a number of official documents and declarations. For instance, in the *Document on the European Identity*, published on 14 December 1973 in Copenhagen, the Nine Foreign Ministers of the EC emphasised their intention:

> "to play an active role in world affairs and thus to contribute, in accordance with the purposes and principles of the United Nations Charter, to ensuring that international relations have a more just basis; that the independence and equality of the states are better preserved; that prosperity is equitably shared; and that the security of each country is more effectively guaranteed" (European Community 1998, 51).

When formulating a common policy towards third countries, the EC agreed on acting in accordance with the following principles:

"a) The Nine, acting as single entity, will strive to promote harmonious and constructive relationships with these countries. (...)

b) In the future when the Nine negotiate collectively with other countries, the institutions and procedures chosen should enable the distinct character European identity to be respected

c) In bilateral contacts with other countries, the member states of the Community will increasingly act on the basis of agreed common positions" (European Community 1998, 51-52).

Since the publication of the Document on the European Identity, the EU has repeatedly expressed this stance in innumerable EU Declarations. For instance, the Title V of the Treaty on European Union (TEU), which introduced the Common Foreign and Security Policy as a separate pillar, declares that the main objectives of the European foreign policy cooperation are:

"- to safeguard the common values and fundamental interests, independence and integrity of the Union in conformity with the principles of the United Nations Charter;

- to strengthen the security of the Union in all ways;

- to preserve peace and strengthen international security, in accordance with the principles of the United Nations Charter, as well as the principles of the Helsinki Final Act and the objectives of the Paris Charter, including those on external borders;

- to promote international cooperation;

- to develop democracy and the rule of law, and respect for human rights and fundamental freedoms" (Treaty on European Union 1992, Title V, Art. J.1.2).

Here, the idea of the promotion of "common values", which are closely associated with the principles of the United Nations (UN) Charter, is declared as the principal objective of the EU. Defending and promoting the prescribed values such as democracy and human rights continue to occupy a high-ranking position in EU foreign policy formulation. The advancing jurisdiction of international politics through enhancement of international law is still an indispensable element of the Union's conception of order. In other words, in international relations, the EU privileges the rule of law over other power instruments.

This motivation has been repeated in several official declarations of the Commission, the Parliament and the Council as well. At a speech given at the Danish Institute of International Affairs in May 2002, EU High Representative of the CFSP, Javier Solana, defines the elimination of poverty and engagement for peace and stability as the Union's chief moral obligations stemming from European "interests, values and history." The instruments to be applied here are financial assistance, diplomacy and trade as well as multilateral cooperation. Defining the EU as "an instinctive multilateral actor", Solana reemphasises the Union's strong attachment to constructive multilateral mechanism:

> "Our vision, the European vision, is one that combines globalisation with multilateralism in all respects so that every state – however big or small – every individual – however rich or poor – has a stake in his or her own future. That is the route to a fair and just world, but also to a secure world" (Solana 2002, 6).

Again at the same speech, Solana points out the willingness of the European Union, which he defines as "an attractive pole of stability, democracy and prosperity", to maximise its "status as a net exporter of stability by acknowledging legitimate aspirations to join our Union; while emphasising that this is dependent on a commitment to our common values." Here, international cooperation, the engagement of other actors and regional groupings, and international dialogue are identified as essential foreign policy tools (Solana 2002, 2-6).

All these principles are repeated in Treaty of Lisbon which was adopted for the amendment of the TEU and Treaty establishing the European Community. In Treaty of Lisbon, the EU member states declare the international identity of the EU in a more explicit way. The Union's objectives are clearly identified and the text puts special emphasis on enhancing relations with neighbouring countries. Article 10 A of the Treaty of Lisbon is entirely devoted to explaining how the EU conceptualizes its role in world politics with a major focus on foreign policy goals and instruments to achieve the desired goals.

An interesting aspect of Article 10 A is that member states make a clear linkage between values on which the European project is based and the principles the Union seeks to promote abroad. In other words:

" 1. The Union's action on the international scene shall be guided by the principles which have inspired its own creation, development and enlargement, and which it seeks to advance in the wider world: democracy, the rule of law, the universality and indivisibility of human rights and fundamental freedoms, respect for human dignity, the principles of equality and solidarity, and respect for the principles of the United Nations Charter and international law. The Union shall seek to develop relations and build partnerships with third countries, and international, regional or global organisations which share the principles referred to in the first subparagraph. It shall promote multilateral solutions to common problems, in particular in the framework of the United Nations" (Art. 10 A).

The member states agreed that external relations will be based on commonly accepted policies and the EU shall seek closer cooperation with third countries in various policy areas. In its relations with the wider world, the Union shall respect the following principles:

"(a) safeguard its values, fundamental interests, security, independence and integrity;

(b) consolidate and support democracy, the rule of law, human rights and the principles of international law;

(c) preserve peace, prevent conflicts and strengthen international security, in accordance with the purposes and principles of the United Nations Charter with the principles of the Helsinki Final Act and with the aims of the Charter of Paris, including those relating to external borders;

(d) foster the sustainable economic, social and environmental development of developing countries, with the primary aim of eradicating poverty;

(e) encourage the integration of all countries into the world economy, including through the progressive abolition of restrictions on international trade;

(f) help develop international measures to preserve and improve the quality of the environment and the sustainable management of global natural resources, in order to ensure sustainable development; (g) assist populations, countries and regions confronting natural or man-made disasters; and

(h) promote an international system based on stronger multilateral cooperation and good global governance" (Art. 21, 2).

In brief, the self-characterisation of the EU provides explicit indications of its civilian power nature. The remaining question is whether the foreign policy behaviour of the EU resembles to that of a civilian power.

### 2.2.2. The foreign policy behaviour of the EU

Based on the existing literature on civilian power concept, all elements that are identified as crucial for identifying civilian powers can be brought into two broad categories: Objectives and means including diplomacy, persuasion and negotiation methods. Therefore, this part of the study examines to what extent EU can pursue policies in accordance with its prescribed principles. Maull et al. (1997)[7] identified the promotion of universal values such as democracy, human rights, peace and economic development as significant role that the identity of a civilian power implies. Furthermore, use of diplomatic means and negotiation are important features of a civilian power.

One of the most important features of a civilian power is the *commitment to diplomacy* to which the EU attaches great value in its activities outside its borders. Hocking argues that over the years the EU has developed a "multi-layered politico-diplomatic environment" (Hocking 2004, 91) Indeed, since its birth in the 1950s, the EU has built up a specific form of diplomacy using institutionalised dialogue with various states around the world. Even in 1973, the Euro-Arab Dialogue (EAD), which born of a French initiative, was established at the European Council in Copenhagen. In the meetings followed, the two sides, despite their overwhelming political differences, agreed on a closer cooperation in areas such as industry, agriculture, science, education, technology, financial cooperation and infrastructure (Noor 2004, 29-31).

Regarding interregional dialogue, the EU has developed a longstanding institutional dialogue with the Asia-Pacific Region. With the establishment of the Association of South East Asian Nations (ASEAN), which encompasses ten

---

[7] See also Dembinski (2002).

South East Asian countries, the EU sought to enhance its political and economic cooperation with the region through ministerial meetings. Cooperation between the EU and ASEAN is based on a Cooperation Agreement signed in 1980, within little more than a year of the first official meeting of foreign ministers. Besides, on a bilateral level, the EU has opened negotiations for agreements with Thailand and Singapore with the intention of strengthening its dialogue with all of the interested countries in the region (Loewen 2006, 2-3).

In addition, the EU has intensified its interregional dialogue with partners such as the Gulf Cooperation Council, countries in the Baltic Sea and Arctic Sea regions, African, Caribbean and Pacific (ACP) nations as well as with South Asian countries in a number of economic, political and cultural areas. Similarly significant is the Union's dialogue with partners of the Southern Mediterranean partners, which was strengthened with the launch of Euro-Mediterranean Partnership (EMP). A wide framework for political, economic and social relations between the EU and the countries of the Mediterranean, the Euro-Mediterranean Partnership (or the Barcelona Process) serves as an evidence for the Union's strong attachment to the reinforcement of political and security dialogue, economic and financial partnership and, above all, to bilateral and multilateral agreements (Tanner 2002, 4-5).

In short, the Union's pursuit of a unique form of diplomacy, along with its willingness to constitute institutionalised dialogue and cooperation with both individual states and regions outside its borders demonstrate the applicability of the civilian power concept to the analysis of EU's foreign policy activity. This can be seen in Whitman's own assertion that "the notion of civilian power (…) represents a touch-stone for debates on the international role of the EU because of the premise that it is conducting a distinctive form of diplomacy, in both form and substance" (Whitman 2002, 4).

The second criterion to be discussed is the *use of economic instruments* in the pursuit of foreign policy objectives and interests. Smith argues that economic instruments allude to the promise of aid, the aid itself, sanctions and other means (Smith 2005, 4). Indeed, humanitarian aid has always occupied, and still occupies a key position in Union's external relations. Through the European Community Humanitarian Aid Department (ECHO), set up in 1992, the EU is the world's main player in this field. According to the Annual Review 2006 released by the European Commission, with a budget of more than € 500 million a year, the Humanitarian Aid Department makes a crucial financial contribution to a wide range of humanitarian projects. The EU, in close cooperation with non-governmental organisations, UN specialised agencies and other international organisations, provides the victims with essential equipment and food in case of emergency, provides rescue teams, funds emergency hospitals and install temporary communications systems. The major crisis zones where EU operates include Nepal, Afghanistan, the Palestinian Authority, the Democratic Republic of Congo, Colombia, the Horn of Africa and the Northern Caucasus.

The application of economic instruments encompasses the Union's relations with former colonies in ACP as well. The regularly adjusted and updated Lomé Convention, which set out the principles of the Union with regard to its cooperation with ACP countries, gave the Development Cooperation Policy a legal basis. With the first three Lomè Conventions, the primary emphasis was placed on economic development and non-reciprocal trade benefits for ACP states including unlimited entry to the EC for 99% of industrial goods and many other products. Until the end of the 1980s, the EU Development Policy was politically unconditional. With the Lomé IV, however, the partners agreed to set a "human rights clause" as a fundamental part of the cooperation. At the Lomé IV revision in 1995, the essential nature of the human rights clause as a condition for further cooperation was reemphasised, implying that any violation of human rights could result in partial or total suspension of the development aid provided by the EU. This was also the first time that the European Development Fund was not increased (Gerrick 2004, 131-134).

Smith defines it as a "conditionality", which "is now a well-established feature of EU foreign relations" (Smith 2005, 4). She differentiates "positive conditionality" from "negative conditionality" by implying that the former requires promising benefits to a country when it fulfils the requirements. The latter, on the other hand, includes reduction and even suspension of such benefits when the country violates the prescribed conditions (Smith 2005, 18). According to Smith, the EU uses positive conditionality by promising agreements, loans, aid, and dialogue as long as the partners fulfil certain political and economic requirements which were set in advance. Smith asserts that, positive conditionality is the most desirable method for the EU, despite the difficulties caused by the delivery of incentives and reluctance to include agricultural products in its free trade agreements with non-EU countries. In spite of the drawback of positive conditionality, Smith finds the application of negative conditionality by the Union more problematic because of the inability of the member states to agree on taking firm measures against the external partner states. Smith sums up these doubts by stating that, "This is due mostly to calculations of the relative strategic and commercial importance of targeted countries, but is also – to be fair – due to serious doubts within the EU about the merits of applying sanctions or negative measures" (Smith 2005, 11).

Smith's negative conditionality resembles the notion of "negative transference instrument" used by Whitman with a reference to the economic sanctions imposed by the EU. Different from Smith, Whitman regards sanctions as one of the four foreign policy instruments that the EU has developed that "offer support for the notion that the EU still acts as a civilian power" (Whitman 2002, 14).

*Commitment to multilateralism* is a further characteristic of civilian power. As mentioned above, a civilian power is an opponent of unilateral action and pursues foreign policy based on multilateral instruments, collective action and compromise. The question is to what extent the principle of multilateralism determines the Union's actions in the changing nature of international relations.

It is commonly acknowledged in International Relations studies that the geostrategic, political and economic changes in the post Cold War environment as well as global threats such as terrorism and the proliferation of weapons of mass destruction have changed the global security agenda drastically, revealing the need to handle important world affairs in a collective way (Maull 1990, 93). In this changing international relations environment, the Union reaffirms its commitment to multilateralism, and engagement for the juridification of international relations by strengthening the role of international organisations such as the United Nations. In *European Security Strategy*, adopted by the

European Council in 2003, Javier Solana introduces the term "effective multi-lateralism" as the core element of the European approach to international affairs:

> "In a world of global threats, global markets and global media, our security and prosperity increasingly depend on an effective multilateral system. The development of a stronger international society, well functioning international institutions and a rule-based international order is our objective. We are committed to upholding and developing International Law" (European Security Strategy 2003, 9).

The heart of this "effective multilateral system" is the United Nations which "has the primary responsibility for the maintenance of international peace and security." Thus, "strengthening the United Nations, equipping it to fulfil its responsibilities and to act effectively, is a European priority" (European Security Strategy 2003, 9).

Council Decision *94/800/EC* concerning the adoption of World Trade Organisation (WTO) agreements reached in the Uruguay Round multilateral negotiations (1986-1994) is a further example of the Union's commitment to multilateral solutions. Likewise, at the Göteborg European Council of June 2001, the EU member states, with reference to the challenge posed by the proliferation of ballistic missiles, stressed the need for strengthening international norms and political instruments, and invited the international community to global and multilateral action (Annex I). Similarly, in 2003 the Commission presented the Council and the European Parliament with a Communication called *The European Union and the United Nations: the choice of multilateralism*, which calls multilateralism as a fundamental feature of EU international relations. Commission emphasizes the growing need to seek collective solutions to global problems and calls for the enhancement of international organizations. The text points out the Union's readiness to bind itself to international principles, for respecting global rules would enable the world to create the necessary conditions for sustainable peace. In this regard, the Commission reiterates its commitment to the UN, which is called as the guarantor of multilateralism in the world. The text also emphasizes the need to protect the UN system against the violent attacks on its personnel and general system.

*The promoter of democracy, human rights, peace and development* is another role that the identity of a civilian power implies. In the rhetoric of EU representatives and various EU Declarations, the EU gives special emphasis to development, peace, democracy promotion and human rights. In the draft of the Constitutional Treaty, the Union both constructs a European identity and specifies its responsibilities to the external world in the following way:

> "In its relations with the wider world, the Union shall uphold and promote its values and interests. It shall contribute to peace, security, sustainable development of the Earth, solidarity and mutual respect among peoples, free and fair trade, eradication of poverty and protection of human rights, in particular the rights of the children as well as to the strict observance and the development of international law, including respect for the principles of the United Nations Charter" (Treaty Title I, Art. I - 3.4).

Indeed, the EU is one of the biggest aid donors in the world. According to figures provided by EC Humanitarian Aid Department, in 2005, the member states provided approximately € 43 billion of aid to developing countries, which is higher than the per capita aid levels of the United States or Japan. Although only four countries have reached the UN target value of 0.7 % of their Gross National Product (GNP), the EU continues to fund thousands of development projects all over the world. For instance, with the contributions from its member states, the EU provides more than 50 % of the total aid provided to the ACP countries in the international community. Also, through the removal of a tariff on all exports of the 49 least-developed countries (with the sole exception of arms); the EU aims at accelerating the economic development and the integration process in the region (Wolf 2003, 7).

In order to place the protection of human rights and the promotion of democracy at the heart of its foreign policy objectives, the EU wields numerous instruments. In 2006 The European Parliament and the Council adopted *Regulation 1889/2006 on establishing a financing instrument for the promotion of democracy and human rights worldwide*, in which they specified the instrument through which the EU would promote human rights and democracy. These include cooperation and assistance programmes, declarations and demarches, and election observations to foster democratisation efforts in third countries. Regarding the "human rights clause", the EU defines respect for

human rights and democratic principles as an essential provision for cooperation and association agreements with the partner states. In 1994 various
funds specifically dealing with human rights and democratisation issues were
consolidated under one budget heading, the European Initiative for Democracy and Human Rights (EIDHR). According to the *Commission Staff Working
Document* (2001), the European Commission provided nearly €100 million for
147 democracy and human rights projects in 2000 through EIDHR (4).

Nevertheless, the EU is criticised for sacrificing its proclaimed values and objectives for its commercial and security interests, which creates an inconsistent and incoherent human rights policy. Giving the Union's relations with
China as an example, Dembinski argues that regarding human rights violation
cases, the EU sanctions a weaker country sooner than a stronger or strategically significant one (Dembinski 2002, 12-13). Smith, on the other hand,
points out the Union's inconsistent way of imposing negative measures, because of the commercial and strategic ties of one or more member states with
the countries in question (Smith 2005, 11).

Regardless of all this criticism, the European Union, with both its self-characterisation and foreign policy conduct, comes close to an ideal civilian power,
using civilian means, pursing civilian ends and using civilian ways when applying its civilian means. The next step of the study is to outline the debate
whether the use of force invalidates the idea of civilian power Europe.

## 2.3. Civilian Power Europe and the use of force

The creation of European Security and Defence Policy (ESDP) and the Petersberg Declaration in 1992, which are both parts of the CFSP of the European Union, brought about an academic debate about the applicability of the
civilian power concept to the European case (Smith 2000; Burckhardt 2004;
Bretherton et al. 2006). One view argues that the notion of CPE is no longer
valid because of the current militarization of the EU. The contrasting view,
however, claims that "thanks to the militarising of the Union, the latter might at
long last be able to act as a real power in the world and more importantly as a
real civilian power" (Stavridis 2001, 2).

The first view represented by Karen Smith argues that civilian power concept is no longer applicable to the EU as a result of the Union's efforts to increase its military might. Smith argues that the EU "despite the obvious current weaknesses of (its) defence dimension (...) is now abandoning its civilian power image" (Smith 2000, 12). While stressing the civilian nature of the Stability Pact for Southern-Eastern Europe and the Enlargement Process, Smith expresses her concerns about the recent military movements that have called into question the applicability of the concept to the EU case. Defining the outcome of the humanitarian mission on Somalia as a catastrophic example of its kind, Smith warns that "peacekeeping and humanitarian missions may not be, or remain, even primarily "civilian" in nature." The use of force may be an essential instrument for the success of the military mission, but where a mission passes from a civilian to a military one is vague. Thus, if "we define peacekeepers as a military instrument (...) an actor possessing this instrument is not a pure civilian power" (Smith 2000, 9). The argument made here is that collective defence – in which the EU is not involved – is much more civilian in nature than the use of force for intervention reasons since intervention might be regarded as an attempt to pursue interests (Smith 2000, 24).

Smith's view is shared by several other scholars. Sjursen (2004), for instance, asserts that the current militarization of the EU initiated a debate concerning to what extent values are compatible with military might. The main argument made by Sjursen is that it has become difficult for scholars to theoretically deal with security issues from a view based on values. In other words, Sjursen argues that literature on EU external relations face the problem as regards how to situate values within contemporary evolution of the security dimension of EU external relations. Schorlemer has similar concerns when suggesting that participating in peace-making missions could seriously call into question the civilian nature of the activity. For Schorlemer, though intervention is justified by humanitarian reasons such peace-keeping interventions are mostly carried out by a stronger state against a weaker state, which Schorlemer calls as "interventionismus à la carte" (Schorlemer 2000, 47; Burckhardt 2004, 12). Others also argue that the tasks of forces falling into the scope of Petersberg tasks, such as crisis management and peace-making contradicts one of the most prominent objectives of a civilian power, namely, commitment to international law. Jünemann et al. (2002) argue that certain humanitarian practices such as sending back of refugees or various measures to prevent catastrophic events do not present a legal problem and they require no UN –Mandate. However, peace keeping missions are problematic in terms of international law (Jünemann et al. 2000, 38-39). Therefore, EU activities within the framework of Petersberg Task present problems for the CPE (Burckhardt 2004). Thus, the first view sees "the build up of the CFSP and particularly the ESDP not as the beginning of a "real", but as the "end" of a Civilian Power Europe" (Burckhardt 2004, 12).

The proponents of the other argument primarily refer to the second element of Maull's definition of civilian power (Smith 2004), especially his identification of the military power "as a residual instrument serving essentially to safeguard other means of international interaction" (Maull 1990, 93). Their argument is also on built on Maull's article that analyzes the case of Germany following its military involvement in the 1999 Kosovo War. For Maull, even after the deployment of its military forces outside the NATO area, Germany still remains a civilian power because it chose "solidarity and the promotion of human rights over its desire to avoid the use of force" (Maull 1999, 6). Maull also implies Germany's commitment to the foreign policy orientation of an ideal civilian power during the Kosovo war by stating that:

> "German attitudes and policies towards Kosovo were driven by concern about the atrocities there. (…) Germany also led diplomatic efforts to consider ways to reconstruct and stabilise the war-torn Balkans. German policies were policies in pursuit of values and norms, rather than short term interests. (…) Germany was also in the forefront of searching for political alternatives to the war" (Maull 1999, 27-28).

Similarly, Stavridis argues that using military means does not contradict the concept of civilian power Europe. Challenging the view that the creation of ESDP marked the end of the applicability of the concept, Stavridis considers the Union's militarization as "an opportunity for the EU to act as a real civilian power, i.e. an international actor that effectively promotes democratic principles in the world" (Stavridis 2001, 5). For him, the use of military means can be an essential tool in the pursuit of civilian ends, such as democracy and human rights.

In the same way, Whitman takes the view that "developing and strengthening the military instrument is not sufficient to validate or invalidate the notion of civilian power Europe" (Whitman 2002, 19). Here, Whitman points out that the evolution of ESDP does not contradict the nature of the civilian power concept since the EU still promotes civilian power instruments and refrains from employing military power. Moreover, the Petersberg tasks that contain humanitarian and peacekeeping elements giving the EU a "civilian power military posture" (Whitman 2002, 21), because "the Petersberg orientation of policy area is in conformity with the civilian power norms" (Whitman 2002, 24). Therefore, from this point of view a civilian power should not worry about the means, but about the ends of its foreign policy (Burckhardt 2004).

To put it briefly, though the creation of the ESDP has raised an academic debate over the suitability of the civilian power concept for the European Union, the argument that the use of force is not sufficient to invalidate the civilian power Europe seems more convincing than the contrasting view supported by Smith. Indeed, with regard to regional conflicts, such as that in the Middle East, the Union still privileges diplomatic and multilateral arrangements over military solutions.

## 2.4.    Why does the EU operate as a civilian power?[8]

### 2.4.1. The realist explanation

Realism is undoubtedly one of the main theoretical schools of IR. Its significance for IR studies lies in that realism has deep roots in ancient philosophy

---

[8] This chapter is based on Dembinski (2002). See also Burckhardt (2004). The theoretical distinction of the international relations schools to understand the roots of the CPE as well as the line and logic of arguments are put forward in Dembinski's (2002) article. Dembinski discusses the following theoretical standpoints: realism, rationalism, constructivism and liberal institutionalism. However, for the development of my argument, I will discuss the realist perspective, the constructivist perspective (since these two are the main theoretical views adopted by scholars researching on CPE) and the institutionalist perspective; the latter forming the theoretical background of this study's analysis.

and that it has so far provided fruitful insights into foreign policy analysis (Burchill 1996, 67). Realists take states as central actors in international politics and grant little role to international organizations. State is the key actor and authority in international relations and realism regards it as the only force that can decide on and shape inter-state cooperation within institutions. Traditional realists argue that state interests are the major determinants of the international system and they define interests with reference to power. In other words, according to the realist view, power is a central instrument used by the nation states in foreign policy. At the same time, nation-states are in search of power when operating in the international system (Burchill 1996, 67-73; Ari 2006, 170). Hans Morgenthau argues that power, which determines the position of the nation-states on the international arena, can be defined both in qualitative and quantitative terms. Accordingly, quantitative factors encompass geography, natural resources, industrial capacity and economic development, population and military might; qualitative factors, on the other hand, include national morale and character as well as the quality of diplomacy and government (112-149). Yet, in academic literature, a high-priority is given to the military and economic power capacity of nation-states (Burchill 1996, 67-73; Ari 2006, 170).

As Dembinski (2002) also points out one of the most common explanations for the reasons of the EU's civilian power chapter is the realist perspective. Scholars agree that concerning industrial and economic might, the EU is undoubtedly a vital actor in international politics. However, there are still uncertainties about the extent to which the EU is capable of becoming a real military power (Smith 2000; Burckhardt 2004). Although one of the key objectives of the European Integration process was the establishment of a European Defence Community (EDC) to counterbalance the irresistible military ascendancy of the Soviet Union in Europe, all these attempts to create a supranational European army have failed (Bertram et al. 2002, 11). Smith argues that a wide range of "factors blocked the development of a purely European defence identity, most of which had little to do with any intrinsic merits of civilian power." Smith argues that the Union's inability to increase its military power resulted primarily from its unwillingness to act against the United States.

Therefore, the EU is a civilian power not by conviction, but "by default" (2000: 14).

In fact, Duchêne already defined that the EC as a "civilian group of countries long on economic power and relatively short on armed force" (Duchêne 1973, 19). Following the same manner of reasoning, Robert Kagan claims that the EU's attachment to treaties, the rule of law and multilateralism results primarily from its military incapability and weakness:

> "Europe's military weakness has produced a perfectly understandable aversion to the exercise of military power. Indeed, it has produced a powerful European interest in inhabiting a world where strength doesn't matter, where international law and international institutions predominate, where unilateral action by powerful nations is forbidden, where all nations regardless of their strength have equal rights and are equally protected by commonly agreed-upon international rules of behaviour....If Europe's strategic culture today places less value on power and military strength and more value on such soft-power tools as economics and trade, isn't it partly because Europe is militarily weak and economically strong?" (Kagan 2002, 9-12)

Kagan argues that, despite their complaints about the American tendency to unilateralism in international affairs, the Europeans show neither ambition for power, nor desire to go back to the power politics of the eighteenth- and nineteenth-century European empires, and confine their foreign policy actions to declarations, treaties and multilateral instruments. Kagan points out that the military weakness of the EU becomes more evident when it comes to military interventions outside its territories as it was the case during the Balkan War when "the European role was limited to providing peacekeeping forces after the United States had, largely on its own, carried out the decisive phases of a military mission and stabilized the situation" (Kagan 2002, 7).

Taking an opposing view, Robert Cooper (2003) defines the devastating experiences of history, especially those of Germany, Italy, Greece and Spain, as the chief reason for the declining defence budgets of the EU in the last decade. For the Europeans, who prefer to live in world where law rules rather than one of power relations, the use of military power has low legitimacy. Cooper adds by saying that the EU, comprised of democratic societies, promotes pluralism and the rule of law in domestic affairs, and aims at promoting these values on the international scene as well. Therefore, Kagan's line of reasoning is inadequate for explaining the EU preference for multilateral arrangements and negotiation based on international law.

Dembinski (2002) and Burckhardt (2004) argue that since realism focuses almost exclusively on military might, one might wonder how the Union would behave if member states acquired military capabilities. Therefore, these scholars conclude that realist explanation fails to account for the reason behind the civilian nature of European foreign policy behavior. Indeed, even if the EU had an army under a single European commander, it would still need a central authority that is responsible for making decisions concerning the deployment of military forces.

### 2.4.2. The normative explanation

The second view put forward by Dembinski (2002) is the normative explanation. As Dembinski (2002) and Burckhardt (2004) also point out the normative aspect of civilian power Europe is based upon the ideas of Manners, who introduced the normative power Europe (NPE) concept in his 2002 article. Since 2002, the NPE concept has become a major reference work in academic literature on EU external relations.

Manners argued that the EU is a unique type of actor, whose distinctiveness results primarily from three features intrinsic to the EU. These are the EU's rejection of divisive nationalism and war-torn centuries, its hybrid governance structures and its constitutional formation (240-241). Manners puts forward five core values - peace, liberty, democracy, the rule of law and respect for human rights - and four subsidiary values - social solidarity, anti-discrimination, sustainable development and good governance - that are embedded in the treaties and the activities of the Union in the international arena.

Manners identifies the Union's opposition to the death penalty as an important example of its commitment to promote its values externally (Manners 2002, 240). Regarding the EU activity in human rights issues generally and the death penalty in particular, Manners suggests that:

"not only is the EU constructed on a normative basis, but importantly that it predisposes it to act in a normative way in world politics. It is built upon the crucial and usually overlooked observation that the most important factor shaping the international role of the EU is not that what it does or what it says, but what it is" (Manners 2002, 251).

Manners comes to the conclusion that "we cannot overlook the extent to which the EU is normatively different to other polities" (Manners 2002, 241). Dembinski (2002) questions the main motivation behind the EU's norm-oriented foreign policy conduct and identifies the democratic peace theory and role-theory as two main explanations about the root causes of the NPE. The next section addresses this topic.

### 2.4.2.1. Democratic peace theory

As Farnham (2003) summarizes, according to the proponents of democratic peace theory democratic states display less inclination to wage war against each other and act more peacefully than autocratic regimes. This results primarily from the utilitarian calculations of the citizenry, institutional obstacles and norms. The institutional explanation of the democratic peace theory argues that "due to the complexity of the democratic process and the requirement of securing a broad base of support for risky policies, democratic leaders are reluctant to wage wars, except in cases wherein war seems a necessity or when the war aims are seen as justifying the mobilization costs" (Maoz and Russett quoted in: Farnham 2003, 397).

The second assumption of the democratic peace theory points out since democracies adopt normative principles in the domestic arena, they are more likely to externalise their domestic values and norms in international relations when they are convinced that these ideational factors are also accepted by other nations. With the help of these reciprocally respected norms, actors rely on instruments such as negotiation and diplomacy and refrain from acting in a violent manner. "All these factors lessen the risk that one democracy will attack another" (Farnham 2003, 397).

When applied to the European Union, the democracy peace theory contends that EU formulates foreign policies based normative principles provided all member states respect norm in the domestic arena (Dembinski 2002, 18-19; Burckhardt 2004, 16). Therefore, Dembinski (2002) and Burckhardt (2004) argue that the domestic adoption of values and norms makes the EU a civilian power. Here, these authors refer to Wagner et al. (2003) who point to a reciprocal relationship between internal and external system. In their study, Wagner et al. contend that the historical experiences of EU member states have played an important role in international relations of the European countries. The main argument here is that since Europe was for centuries a continent of wars and violent conflicts, European leaders have sought solutions that would end hostilities and bring about peaceful relations among their countries. Therefore, they accepted a wide range of normative principles that would regulate interstate relations in Europe. This process gradually led to "civilized" relations in the continent and Europe has become a continent of peace. Wagner et al. argue that norms not only determine relations between European countries, but they also form the basis for Europe's policies towards third countries. They argue that Europe's attitude towards minority issues in Eastern European countries shows the linkage between domestic and internal politics. Because European countries respect minority rights at home, they also promote such norms in their relations with non-European countries (Wagner et al. 2003, 590-592).

However, as Farnham rightly observes, the democratic peace theory puts its primary emphasis on relations among democratic countries and fails to account for how those states with a democratic political culture would act towards non-democratic state. Thus, Farnham questions whether democratic countries are expected to apply the same negotiating standards to all states regardless of their regime types (Farnham 2003, 407-408). The same question applies to EU external relations: Should we expect the EU democracies to behave in the same way in its relations with third countries lacking democratic regime forms?

Scholars have argued and showed that the internal adoption of normative principles does not necessarily mean that normative arrangements would determine behaviour in the international arena. As already mentioned above, according to the democratic peace theory, democratic nations avoid disputes and prefer peaceful solutions over physical violence. However, several scholars contend that democratic nations fail to act in accordance with what is expected from them (Dembinski 2002, 19; Burckhardt 2004, 17). Indeed, a considerable number of empirical studies empirically demonstrate that democracies establish peaceful relations only with other democracies and they are aggressive in their relations with autocracies. In other words, there is "a dualism in a democracy's foreign conduct with one set of norms characterizing its relations with other democracies and another set applying to those with non-democracies" (Chan quoted in Farnham 2003, 408).

Referring to Dixon (1994), Dembinski (2002) and Burckhardt (2004) also argue that although its reference to the reciprocal relationship between internal structures and external behaviour is of interest, the democratic peace theory says little about why democratic states are expected to apply the same normative standards in internal and external politics. Foreign policy "is especially characterized by concerns for national sovereignty, security, identity, and the like" and democratic peace theory fails to account for why one might expect foreign policy behaviour to be "nothing more than an extension of domestic politics" (Dixon 1994: 17). Therefore, democratic peace theory provides no satisfactory explanation for the root causes of CPE.

### 2.4.2.2. The constructivist explanation

Role-theory is the second explanation for the normative basis for CPE. Dembinski and Burckhardt (2004) refer to Kirste et al. (1996), along with others, and argue that their model serves as the basis for explaining the impact of identity on state behaviour. What is role-theory according to Kirste et al.? Role-theory is an actor-oriented approach to explain divergences in foreign policy conduct of states by focusing on two main factors. Accordingly, Kirste et al. argue that the nature of a particular actor (here actor refers to states operating in the international realm) is determined both by the individual elements on the actor level (ego-part) and by the factors on the system level (alter-part) (Kirste et al. 1996, 289). To put it differently, the ego-part alludes to the self-conception; that is to say common norms and values that are learned through socialisation process and widely shared by the national decision-makers. The alter-part on the other hand, is constructed by the surrounding conditions and the expectations of other actors on the system level. The ego- and alter-part construct a specific and diversified pattern of role-concept which is a mixture of geographical, historical and socio-economic features as well as power politics and system structures. With time, role-concepts shape the role behaviour of individual states. Here, role behaviour implies the actual behaviour of the national role-bearers in concrete situations of foreign policy interaction (Kirste and Maul 1996, 292-297).

Dembinski (2002) and Burckhardt (2004) point to the following weaknesses of the role-theory: As already mentioned, the civilian norms and values have been repeated in several EU documents and statements. However, there are still uncertainties as regards to what extent EU member states have suc-ceeded in constructing a political identity, which might act as ego-part that Kirste et al. put forward (Burckhardt 2004). Burckhardt refers to Whitman (1998) and argues that public opinion gives no indication of a shared civilian power identity. Whitman asserts that though member states have gradually formulated a common "international identity" (27), it seems debatable whether European identity is stronger than national identities. Whitman suggests that one might observe "indications of a shared conception of being part of a European political community that are identifiable across the peoples of the Union" (189), yet public opinion surveys demonstrate that national identities still maintain their primacy in peoples' minds. Whereas Germany, Spain, Por-tugal and Ireland are less supportive of an EU with stronger military capabili-ties, others such as United Kingdom, France and Belgium prefer closer coop-eration within European defence cooperation (Whitman 1998, 192). There-fore, certain countries come closer the foreign policy orientation of civilian power, whilst others favour *l'Europe puissance* (Dembinski 2002, 21; Burck-hardt 2004, 19).

Another weakness of role theory is its argument that system level factors such as expectations shape foreign policy identity. Whitman questions "how the international context has contributed to the modification of the interna-tional role of the Union" (Whitman 1998, 33), and argues that since the first steps towards political integration, European countries have formulated their policies in accordance with their collective interests and their understanding of Europe's responsibilities towards the outer world (Whitman 1998, 33). However, scholars argue that there is little empirical evidence suggesting that non-European countries expect the EU to adopt the civilian power identity. Therefore, it seems debatable to what extent CPE is the product of external expectations, which Kirste et al. call the alter-part (Dembinski 2002, 21; Burckhardt 2004, 19).

### 2.4.3. Institutional constraints

Dembinski (2002)[9] proposes a liberal institutionalist view for explaining the origins of civilian power Europe. Accordingly, the question concerns whether the sui generis nature of the EU might help account for the Union's foreign policy activity. Dembinski's argument rests upon the observation that the institutional structure of the EU and the internal decision-making procedures are the main reasons why the EU operates as a civilian power in the international realm (Dembinski 2002, 21-26).

Indeed, in several many studies on the European Union, an accurate distinction is made between the classic "community method" of pillar one and the method used in foreign policy cooperation in pillar two. Indeed, despite the developments in the CFSP, pillar two differs from pillar one in terms of decision-making, its intergovernmental nature and the dominant actors, with the European Parliament and the Commission far weaker in the CFSP than in the EC. Foreign policies are still "primarily national in orientation and generally widely perceived as the one of the ultimate expressions of national sovereignty" (Peterson et al. 1999: 232). Decisions under the Title V are still taken unanimously, qualified majority voting (QMV) only used for the implementation of a common strategy. The decisions on the adoption of common strategies are also taken unanimously by the European Council, particularly in areas where the member states have interests in common. Joint actions and common positions, which do not form the basis of a common strategy, are decided by using QMV; yet the scope of the QMV is limited in that a member

---

[9] See also Burckhardt (2004).

state can still oppose the adoption of common strategies for important reasons of national policy. In such cases, the Council may request that the matter be referred to the European Council for a unanimous decision by the Heads of State or Government. Furthermore, QMV does not apply to decisions with military implications (Peterson et al. 1999, 232).

The intergovernmental structure of the CFSP decision-making process is regarded by Dembinski (2002) as the main obstacle to a consistent and effective foreign policy at the EU level. The principle of unanimity requires all member states to agree upon bringing their individual as well as collective power resources for a common stance. However, this often fails to materialize, if member states have important national interests in the policy area. Moreover, the time required for achieving unanimity presents a serious obstacle when rapid action is needed in crisis situations. There is neither EU foreign minister nor a decision-making body for foreign policy activity at the EU level. An often-quoted example is the failure of the EU to function as a single entity during the war in the Balkans (Missiroli 2002, 4-6).

Moreover, Dembinski (2002) argues that the specific form of diplomacy with institutional dialogue at the heart of it which the EU has built up with the states outside its borders complies with the Union's institutional requirements. The establishment of political, economic and social dialogues with other countries enables all the member states with different national interests to express their opinion at the negotiation table. Again through dialogue, each Member State has the opportunity of exercising power within the negotiation process.

Dembinski (2002) further argues that thanks to short time required and the possibility of predicting its implications, the EU is still interested in the application of economic incentives in its relations with non-EU countries. On the other hand, as Smith (2005) suggests, the EU fails to impose negative sanctions and to agree on taking hard measures towards certain partner states, because some EU member states are reluctant to endanger their political and economic ties with the countries in question.

Similarly, Dembinski (2002) argues that sanctions might have unpredictable results. Therefore, EU member states with close partnerships with certain third countries are reluctant to apply economic and diplomatic sanctions.

Dembinski (2000) also suggests that the Union's preference for multilateralism and international law in its external relations originate from its complex institutional framework. To put it differently, since the EU rests on certain normative principles and rules for the well-functioning of its entire institutional structure, the member states expect third countries to accept this body of shared rules and regulations in order to build partnerships. Therefore, for Dembinski (2000), the Union's inclination to multilateral relations is due to the Community's origins as well as to its continued attempts to instil the rule of law in relations between its member states.

The conclusion that can be drawn from these examples is that the institutional features of the EU and the internal decision-making mechanism are the main reasons for the civilian nature of the EU foreign policy conduct. The intergovernmental nature of CFSP and the obligation to unanimity prevent the EU from giving common rapid reactions to crisis situations, particularly during wars. From this perspective, the foreign policy structure is responsible for the civilian character of the EU, because it makes the more civilian (Burckhardt 2004).

### 2.4.3.1. The European march towards the CFSP

Since the early days of the European Integration, the establishment of a political union, a common foreign policy, and even a common defence policy has been regularly put into the EC/EU agenda through various policy proposals. Between 1951 and 1954, the six founding members negotiated on the Treaty Establishing the European Defence Community which aimed at building common European armed forces under one budget and command. However, this dream never materialised, since the French Parliament refused to ratify the treaty in 1954. During the Cold War, the most intensive negotiations on a closer political cooperation were conducted on the basis of the so-called Fouchet plans of 1960/61. Suggested by France, Fouchet I envisaged a political union of the six members which would be run by an intergovernmental Council. As no consensus could be reached following several drafts submitted by France, negotiations were ended in 1962 for the second time (Knapp et al. 2006, 427-429).

After the failure of the European Defence Community in 1954 and the Fouchet plans during the 1960s, the first practical and tangible steps were taken when the European Political Cooperation mechanism was created after being approved at the Summit in Hague in 1969. The EPC was set up as a forum of the national foreign ministries with the goal of coordinating the national policies of the member states by presenting common reports on specific issues. Nevertheless, in spite of subsequent developments to expand its scope and decision-making mode, the EPC maintained its intergovernmental structure. It had no permanent institutions and the roles of the European Commission and the European Parliament remained extremely limited, which was a precondition for French participation (Mutimer 1990, 7-8).

This non-binding and under-institutionalised nature of the EPC was perceived as a major obstacle to the project of creating a political union. Nevertheless, the EPC was an effective and crucial attempt towards the establishment of a common European foreign policy because "the EPC mechanism allowed the Community to seize on…the simple reality that the Community was far more powerful when it spoke with one voice, instead of six and 12" (Peterson et al. 1999, 226).

It was only with the Single European Act (SEA) of 1987 that the EPC received its legal basis and became part of the European Communities. The SEA re-emphasised the need for a closer European cooperation in the foreign policy field by stating that "The High Contracting Parties, being members of the European Communities, shall endeavour jointly to formulate and implement a European foreign policy" (Title III, Art. 30, point 1). The SEA confirmed the duties of the each institution involved and the procedures of the EPC framework, which remained intergovernmental and required decisions made in a consensual way (Art. 30, points 3-4). The external policies of the EC, as well as the policies decided in the EPC, had to be consistent and the two institutions, the Presidency and the Commission, "shall have special responsibility for ensuring that such consistency is sought and maintained" (Title III, Art. 30, point 5). With the SEA, the member states also decided on the creation of an administrative unit at the General Secretariat of the Council in Brussels, whose duty was to assist the Presidency in the preparation and implementation of the activities of the EPC (Title III, Art. 30, point 10).

With the end of the Cold War and German Reunification, the Twelve, recognizing the significant changes in the security environment created by the dissolution of the Soviet Union, intensified the process of integration in the field of foreign policy cooperation which would allow them to define collective interests and speak with a single voice. Moreover, EC countries also wanted to acquire a more political profile in world affairs (Noor 2004).

With the Treaty of Maastricht (1992), the CFSP was created as the formal constitutional basis for foreign policy cooperation and was incorporated into one single institutional framework. Constituting the "second pillar" of the European Union, the CFSP expanded the scope and depth of decision-making, making the Council the central decision-making body of the CFSP. The common positions defined by the Council on a particular issue required the member states to implement their national policies in accordance with the positions concerned (Art. J 2, point 2). The Treaty confirmed the role of the Commission by stating that it "shall define the principles of and general guidelines for the common foreign and security policy" and "shall take the decisions necessary for defining and implementing the common foreign and security policy on the basis of the general guidelines adopted by the European Council" (Art. J 8, point 1-2).

On the administrative level, despite the lack of a clear definition of the roles of either, the Maastricht Treaty institutionalised exchanges between the Committee of Permanent Representatives (COREPER) and the Political Committee, consisting of Political Directors with CFSP responsibilities of preparing and implementing CFSP policies (Art. J 8, point 5).

The Maastricht Treaty introduced majority voting for the first time on issues covered by CFSP (Art. J 3, point 2). Yet, the scope of qualified majority voting was limited to the implementation of joint actions adopted by the Council. Art. J 3, point 1 states that: "Whenever the Council decides on the principle of joint action, it shall lay down the specific scope, the Union's general and specific objectives in carrying out such action, if necessary its duration, and the means, procedures and conditions for its implementation."

Moreover, because of its intergovernmental nature and the decision-making procedure with the member states as the main actors, the "separate" and "distinct" pillar of the European Union was still outside the legal authority of the Commission and the Parliament. Thus, "for all the intents and purposes the principle of unanimity is unaffected by the treaty" (Stuart 1994, 4). Regardless, the Maastricht Treaty, with its introduction of a CFSP as a separate instrument of the European Union, is widely perceived as a milestone for the European march towards a more united foreign policy (Peterson et al. 1999, 232).

Soon after the Maastricht Treaty, the European continent was confronted with new external threats like the tragic events that occurred in the EU's immediate neighbourhood in ex-Yugoslavia. As a consequence of the weak performance of the EU in that crisis, and many improper decisions taken during nearly four years of civil war, the efficiency and appropriateness of the CFSP were questioned: "The perceived failure of the EU in the Balkans frequently became the foundation for more general indictment of the CFSP and even of the European Integration itself" (Peterson et al. 1999, 239).

In this changed environment, at the European Council of Amsterdam in 1997, many constructive steps were taken to strengthen the effectiveness of the EU institutions and procedures as well as to improve the Union's ability to act as an actor. Regarding the CFSP, the new provisions of Articles 12 and 13 introduced common strategies as a new foreign policy instrument of action, defining the goals, duration and means of a joint action. Common strategies forming "the general framework for actions under the Union's three pillars" were to be implemented by the Council of Foreign Ministers through three ways of decision-making; unanimity for the implementation of guidelines; qualified majority voting for the adoption of decisions applying to a common strategy defined by the European Council as well as to the implementation of a joint action or common position adopted by the Council; and lastly unanimity for decisions with military implications (Peterson et al. 1999, 227).

The creation of the office of the "High Representative" for the CFSP is another important institutional improvement that made a substantial contribution to pillar two decision-making mechanism. With articles 18.3, 26 TEU and Article 207.2 EC, the High Representative, assisting the work of the Council, became responsible for both the management (the formulation, preparation and implementation of CFSP-related decisions) and external representation. In addition, the Policy Planning and Early Warning Unit (PPEWU) at the General Secretariat of the Council was established, which is considered as an essential element for an effective and coherent cooperation in this field.

The launch of the European Security and Defence Policy in 1999 was one of the most remarkable steps towards a more comprehensive, active and operational foreign policy within the EU. More modest than the prior attempts during the 1960s the ESDP no longer intended to create a European army with a single budget and under the command of a single institution. Rather, the member states concentrated on military and civilian means that would improve their ability to deal with the conflicts and instabilities of contemporary world politics. The noteworthy evolution of the ESDP since its launch in 1999 reveals the high priority that the Union has attributed to the security and defence dimension of foreign policy cooperation between the member states.

Although the academic literature on the gradual development of ESDP offers substantial information for the timing and roots of its birth, the reasoning that focuses on the internal dynamics of the progress is the most striking one:

> "ESDP is simply a logical extension of the EU's Common Foreign and Security Policy, which itself arose merely from a recognition that an economic bloc and loose political entity the size of the European Union would inevitably be a global political player. Thus it would need a foreign policy, and a foreign policy is nothing without some kind of defence policy" (Posen 2004, 12).

The Treaty of Nice (2003) introduced the possibility of "enhanced cooperation" for the implementation of joint action or common positions in the CFSP areas, but only if the issues have no military and defence implications. (Art. 27 b) In institutional terms, the Treaty enhanced the role of the Political and Security Committee (PSC), by stating that the Committee "shall monitor the

international situation in the areas covered by the common foreign and security policy and contribute to the definition of policies by delivering opinions to
the Council at the request of the Council or on its own initiative" (Art. 25). Furthermore, with Article 25, the Political and Security Committee shall also play
a role in operations related to crisis management, provided that the Council is
responsible for the monitoring of the process.

Despite these institutional developments in the Union's foreign policy arena,
the CSFP still faces many obstacles and these hamper the EU efforts in increasing its political role in international affairs. The often-quoted problems
are the intergovernmental mechanism of the decision-making procedure in
CFSP-related issues, the limited applicability of majority voting, the lack of
foreign policy instruments and most importantly, the reluctance of nation
states to give up their sovereignty to supranational bodies (Peterson et al.
1999, 243-246).

## 3. The importance of the Middle East for the EU

A combination of factors determines the EU's willingness to strengthen its engagement with the Middle East peace process. These are primarily historical, demographical, geographical and economic reasons (Archick 2005, 3).

Europe's long and multifaceted historical ties with the Middle East still influence its position towards the conflicting parties. Especially owing to ancient religious crusades and the colonial experiences of some European powers in the Arab World during the nineteenth and twentieth centuries, the EU has always been a strategically significant power in the region (Archick 2005, 3). It is also argued that Europe feels itself historically and morally responsible for the creation of the state Israel and the emergence of the Palestinian question:

> "Residual guilt about Europe's colonialist past causes many of its citizens to identify with what they perceive as a struggle for Palestinian freedom against Israeli occupation; at the same time, the Holocaust engenders European support for the security of Israel, but Europeans believe this will only be ensured by peace with the Palestinians" (Archick 2005, 3).

Interestingly, again for historical reasons, the EU member states have diverging interests in the Middle East region and different levels of engagement with the conflict. France, for instance, as a result of its historic linkages with Syria and Lebanon and its close ties to the Maghreb, conducts a more pro-Arab policy. Other Mediterranean EU countries, such as Spain, Greece and Italy have a similar tendency to follow a pro-Palestinian stance. In total contrast, Germany and Netherlands, due mainly to historical and ideological reasons, tend to be more supportive of Israel (Dannreuther 2002, 11).

The geographical proximity of "Europe's Near Abroad" (Dannreuther 2002, 11) makes the encouragement of economic development and political reforms in the region a key concern for the European Union, whose main aim is to guarantee that the problems in the Mediterranean region do not penetrate into the Community. With the European Security Strategy, the Europeans have already pointed to the devastating consequences of "violent and frozen" regional conflicts that "can lead extremism, terrorism and state failure" and at the same time provide "opportunities for organized crime" (4).

The political and economic instability in the region fuels the flow of legal and illegal migration from the Middle East into Europe as well, which adds to EU's already large Muslim population of nearly 15 million. As a result of the enfranchisement of thousands of Muslims in France, Great Britain and Germany, along with the constantly increasing Muslim population in EU capitals, the "Muslim street" in Europe has more weight on domestic politics than the "Arab Streets" in North Africa and the Middle East (Taşpınar 2003). These demographic and geographic trends are also the main reasons for the divergent approaches of the transatlantic partners towards the region (Archick 2005):

> "The presence of nearly 10 million Muslims versus only 700,000 Jews in France and Germany alone helps explain why continental Europe might look at the Middle East from a different angle than does the United States. Indeed, French and German concerns about a unilateral U.S. attack on Iraq or Washington's blind support for Israel are at least partly related to nervousness about the Muslim street at home" (Taşpınar 2003, 76).

Likewise, Europe's economic and trading links to the Middle East region are seen as the main motivation behind the EU's willingness for a more active political role in the peace process (Archick 2003). Due to geographical proximity, the economic ties of many Middle East countries with Europe are closer than any other continent in the world. The EU is traditionally the primary trading partner of all the Middle Eastern states, including Israel. According to the figures provided by EUROSTAT in 2000, the trade flows between EU-15 and MPC- 12 (Mediterranean Partner Countries)[10] were larger in value than the EU-15/China or EU-15/Japan flows. The EU-15 accounted for 45% of total MPC-12 trade in 1999, whereas 8% of the EU-15 trade was with the MPC-12 in 2001.

Moreover, with the launch of a number of programmes that the EU has promoted for the region, such as the Euro-Mediterranean Partnership, the EU aims at enhancing its economic ties with the region. Forming a wide frame-

---

[10] MPC-12: Algeria, Morocco, Tunisia, Egypt, Jordan, Lebanon, Syria, Israel, Palestinian Authority, Cyprus, Malta and Turkey.

work of social, economic and political relations between the member states of the EU and partners of the Southern Mediterranean, EMP aims at the gradual establishment of a free-trade area by 2010.

It is argued that the commercial concerns are the main drivers for the EU Middle East Policy, the primary goal of which is to protect and even strengthen its already strong economic ties with the region. The argument made here is that the financial alignment of the EU with Arab states promotes Israeli suspicions towards the Europeans and deepens its distrust of European good intentions in the peace process. This distrust is pointed out by Dannreuther who states that "Israeli criticisms not only include Europe's perceived pro-Arab line but also the belief that Europe's policies are driven primarily by economic motives, which engender a lack of appreciation of Israel's security concerns" (Dannreuther 2003, 11-12).

To put it briefly, a mixture of factors such as history, demographic trends, geographical closeness and economic interest motivates the EU to increase its political presence in the Middle East peace process. The next part of the study critically assesses the historical development of the EU position towards the Arab-Israeli conflict.

## 4. The EU and the Middle East

The Arab-Israeli conflict, in other words the Middle East conflict, has always occupied a high-ranking position on the agenda of the European Union. The primary objective of the EU is the creation of a secure and stable environment in its immediate neighbourhood. Since the first official declaration following the Yom Kippur War, the EC/EU has continuously announced its commitment to a long lasting and fair peace settlement between the conflicting parties and declared its stance on a number of crucial points as regards the conflict, including Jerusalem, the occupied territories and the use of violence by conflicting parties. As Noor (2004) observes, over the years, the EU has developed its policies consistently and become an influential actor in the peace process. The evolution of the Union's policies towards the region cannot be reduced to the internal dynamics of the conflict or other external factors; rather "EU gradualism (...) is consistent with the process in which the EU, as an economic entity, has evolved over the last many years: a gradual expansion of institutions, membership, parliamentary powers and competencies" (Noor 2004, 24). Nevertheless, many point that despite all institutional developments within foreign policy cooperation, the EU still finds it difficult to formulate common policies towards the conflict. The Union's current status in the MEPP demonstrates that despite its generous financial assistance to the Palestinian Authority (PA) as well as to several other projects, the Union still fails to exert political influence in international peace initiatives (Dannreuther 2002; Renk 2005).

The aim of this section is to critically examine the EU Middle East Policy from its launch in the early 1970s to the 2003 Roadmap. It focuses on the past, present and future status of the EU in the peace process which is closely linked to the historical development of the European foreign policy cooperation. A chronological analysis will serve to better understand how the EU has evolved its role in the MEPP over the years.

## 4.1.  EPC and the Middle East (1971 - 1990)

European Political Cooperation was launched in the wake of the Six-Day War, a war which allowed Israel to substantially increase control over territories compared to 1948. Scholars agree that the war in 1967 drastically changed the balance of power in the Middle East. The dramatic defeat of Egypt during the war was a serious blow to the Pan-Arab-ideology advocated by the Egyptian President Nasser which led to the rise of both Islamic fundamentalism and Palestinian nationalism (Süer et al. 2006, 44-45)

The EC/EU states pursued diverging approaches to the Six-Day war, which were mainly in strong accordance with their national policies towards the region (Greilsammer et al. 1987). France, for instance, considering the Middle East vital for its national interests, was interested in a more active role in the region. Following the war, the French government continuously asserted its support for the Israeli right to exist in a peaceful environment, yet it repeatedly emphasised the legitimate rights of the Palestinians as well. Indeed, the French reaction to the Six-Day War was more critical than other countries of the Community; with the French President Charles de Gaulle condemning Israel explicitly for the war, calling for the Israeli withdrawal from the occupied territories, and imposing an embargo on arms supplies to Israel (Noor 2004, 27).

Although the official stance of West Germany on the Six-Day War was neutral, the general responses to the conflict were mainly pro-Israeli, which can be explained by the historical and moral responsibility of the German people for the State of Israel (Hubel 1992, 42-43).

It can be argued that, these different political reactions within the Community demonstrated the unwillingness and also the inability of the member states to give a common response to an external conflict. Noor puts forward another explanation for the restrictive attitude of the Community during the 1967 War by stating that the EC countries "offered no proposals for settling the conflict, which was largely viewed by observers as a result of Europe's collective consciousness of invasion, trauma, defeat and destruction after the World War II" (Noor 2004, 27).

One of the most important milestones of the European joint action towards the Arab-Israeli conflict was the unanimous adoption of the Schuman Declaration in 1971 by the six European Ministers, which reaffirmed the central character of Resolution 242[11] of the UN Security Council as a basis for peacemaking. The document called for the Israeli withdrawal from the territories occupied during the Six-Day War and recommended the internationalisation of Jerusalem until a proper agreement on a permanent and negotiated solution for the city's status was reached. The EC also proposed to give the Palestinian refugees the choice of either returning to their home or being compensated (Leeuwen 1999, 9).

Meanwhile, having recognized the strategic and economic significance of its trade links with the Mediterranean, the EC introduced the Global Mediterranean Policy (GMP) at the Paris Summit of 21 October 1972 (Noor 2004, 27). The aim was to initiate free trade between the Community and individual Mediterranean states for industrial products (with the exception of some manufactures such as textiles). Also, the member states agreed to give preferential treatment to the export of agricultural products from the Mediterranean countries and offered partial financial aid as well as cohesive treatment of labour force issue. Within the GMP framework, a number of association agreements were signed with Morocco, Algeria, Tunisia, Egypt, Jordan, Syria, and Lebanon (Balbisi et al. 2001, 6).

In October 1973, Egypt and Syria launched a surprise attack on Israel on the Day of Atonement called Yom Kippur, which is one of the holiest and most solemn days of the Jewish community. In response to this unexpected attack, Israeli forces conquered the Golan Heights and advanced into Syria and West of the Suez. Israel's military action changed the regional dynamics se-

---

[11] The UNSC Resolution of 22 November 1967 affirmed that the establishment of a lasting peace requires the application of the following principles: Withdrawal of Israel armed forces from the occupied territories, and respect for and acknowledgment of sovereignty and territorial integrity of all states in the region and their right to live in a peaceful environment. The resolution reemphasised the need for a permanent solution for the refugee problem.

verely, as Arab countries recognized that they were dealing with a new military power in their neighbourhood (Süer et al. 2006, 47).

In opposition to the US full support of Israel, the immediate responses of individual EC states to the Yom Kippur war were more aligned with the Arab side. The installation of an embargo by Arab oil-producing countries against some Western states and quadrupling of oil prices were undoubtedly the most decisive factors in this European pro-Arab orientation because of Europe's heavy dependence on Arab oil at that time (Noor 2004, 28).

In November 1973, the first joint statement on the Middle East issue was issued in Brussels in which the nine foreign ministers for the first time explicitly referred to the "legitimate rights of the Palestinians." With this declaration the EC agreed that a peace settlement should include the following points: "immediate return to the positions held before the war, initiation of peace negotiations with the UN playing a special role in peacemaking and peacekeeping, end to occupation of territories by Israel since 1967, respect for the sovereignty of all states" (Noor 2004, 29).

The European Declaration was welcomed by the Arab states who, as a response, agreed to exempt all European countries except the Netherlands from oil production cutbacks. However, this first attempt of the Community towards a European common approach to the Middle East conflict was perceived by some, especially by Israelis, as an attempt to appease the Arabs. As Dannreuther pinpoints:

"The 1973 war and the subsequent Arab use of the oil weapon had heightened a deep sense of vulnerability, particularly as Europe depended for 80% of its energy supplies from the region as compared to only 12% for the United States. In its subsequent efforts to play a mediatory role in the Arab-Israeli conflict, European diplomacy appeared, at least from an Israeli and US perspective, to place its interests in energy security before those of impartial peacemaking" (Dannreuther 2002, 4).

Nonetheless, the oil embargo of 1973 is a high point in the process of European integration since it gave the Nine the necessary driving force in their efforts to develop a common strategy towards the Arab-Israeli conflict regardless of their diverging interests in the region (Noor 2004, 28). In addition, the oil crisis played an important role in European diplomatic initiatives to invite Yasser Arafat to the UN General Assembly as well as in the UN agreement to give the Palestinian Liberation Organisation (PLO) an observer status (Süer et al. 2006, 28).

### 4.1.1. Euro-Arab Dialogue (1976 - 1980)

The Euro-Arab Dialogue, a joint initiative of the EU and the Arab governments, was established in the aftermath of the 1973 oil embargo and the Arab-Israeli war with the hope of improving relations between the European Union and the Arab States through the promotion of economic and cultural cooperation. Formally launched in 1976, the EAD is regarded as the first attempt of the Community to create a politically structured dialogue with its south-eastern neighbours (Tanner 2002, 4). As Tanner (2002: 2) observes although " this rapprochement did not last, it accelerated the economic multilateralisation of the EC with the Mediterranean." Nevertheless, as a result of the disagreement of the Community and the Arab side on the participation of the Palestine Liberation Organisation, the first meeting of the EAD was postponed a number of times (Miller et al. 2005, 94-95; Noor 2004).

At the first meeting of the General Committee of Euro-Arab dialogue on 20 May 1976, both sides expressed their concern about the dangerous Middle East situation and its threat to international peace. Emphasizing that "the security in Europe is closely linked to the security in the Mediterranean area and that of the Arab region", the partners of the Dialogue declared their commitment to a closer dialogue, in accordance with the principles of the UN Charter. The Palestine question and the crisis in the Middle East were discussed in detail with a consensus that the recognition of the legitimate rights of the Palestinians was a decisive factor for a permanent and peaceful solution to the problem. Additionally, the EC and the Arab governments agreed that the participation of the Palestine Liberation Organisation in all international organisations was a crucial requirement for a long and lasting peace in the region (Noor 2004, 29).

At their second meeting in Tunis on 12 February 1977, the Community and Arab states declared similar positions. After the meeting the EC adopted a communiqué in which the Nine opposed the establishment of Israeli settlements and pointed out the applicability of the Fourth Geneva Convention[12] to the Israeli occupied territories (Noor 2004, 30).

In this period, the Nine repeatedly expressed the Community's stance on the Middle East question through UN debates. At the 32nd UN General Assembly Session, the Belgian Foreign Minister and the President of the Council of the European Community H. Simonet outlined the Community's external policy and presented the EC positions on the Arab-Israeli conflict. Nevertheless, the statement did not go beyond the Community's continued call to put an end to the Israeli occupation of the Palestinian territories (Noor 2004, 30).

A few months after the second meeting of the EAD, in London European Council of June 1977, the EC countries appealed for "the need for a homeland for the Palestinian people" who, together with the representatives of other conflicting parties, "must participate in the negotiations in an appropriate manner to be worked out in consultations between all the parties concerned" (93).

At the third meeting of the General Committee held in Brussels on 28 October 1977, the EC, besides reiterating its previous remarks, invited the Israeli side to act in accordance with the principles of international law and the provisions of the Geneva Convention of 12 August 1949 (Noor 2004, 30).

The Camp David peace process between Egypt and Israel, which began after the unexpected Jerusalem visit of the Egyptian President Anwar el Sadat in November 1977, was conducted bilaterally and with the US President Jimmy Carter acting as the sole arbiter. Although the Camp David Accords, concluded on 17 September 1979, envisaged the establishment of a Palestinian

---

[12] *The Geneva Convention relative to the Protection of Civilian Persons in Time of War* adopted on 12 August 1949 in Geneva set out the minimum provisions that each Party of an armed conflict, not of an international character shall be bound to apply. These include a humanely treatment of all person taking not active part in the hostilities, including the armed forces who have laid down their arms. A discrimination founded on sex, race, colour, religion or faith, birth or wealth, or any similar criteria is also prohibited. (Art. 3)

Autonomy on the West Bank and Gaza as well as a self-governing authority freely elected by the Palestinians, only the decisions concerning Egypt and Israel could be implemented. On the signing of the accord, other Arab States responded to Egypt, one of the historical leaders of the Arab World, by expelling it from the Arab League, leading to the suspension of the Euro-Arab dialogue (Süer et al. 2006, 53).

In spite of the fact that many significant steps were made by both sides during this period of closer cooperation, there was some disagreement on the content and the structure of the dialogue. The EU is criticized for restricting the dialogue to economic gains (attempting to secure its oil supply) and for avoiding a more active political role in the conflict resolution. Navon, for instance, regards the EAD as "a diplomatic fig leaf for a tacit agreement between the EEC and the Arab world", whereby the EEC would support the Arab world diplomatically in the Arab-Israeli conflict and benefit in return from economic agreements and continuous oil supply. Navon even argues that the Arab side used the EAD in its attempts as a vehicle to legitimise the PLO propaganda in Europe as well as "to break the traditional transatlantic solidarity and bring Western Europe into the Arab-Islamic influence". The evidence given is the large-scale immigration from Muslim countries into Europe, the establishment of Arab cultural centres in many European countries and the promotion of Arab language and culture in many capitals of the Community (Navon 2006, 58).

Regardless of this criticism, the launch of the Euro-Arab dialogue is seen as a significant step towards a more comprehensive and effective European Middle East Policy since it created a comprehensive framework for long-term economic and political cooperation between the EC countries and its southern neighbours. The Arab-Israeli conflict and its consequences for the regional stability and security were always on the agenda of the EC and in its contacts with Middle Eastern countries. Nevertheless, due to the failure of EC members to take tangible and practical steps, the position of the Community towards the region is seen as "declaratory" in this period (Noor 2004, 31).

## 4.1.2. Venice Declaration and the first Intifada

The Venice Declaration on the Middle East, adopted at the European Council meeting on 12 June 1980, was undoubtedly the most explicit EC policy statement on the Arab-Israeli conflict up to that time. Issued in the wake of Camp David Accords between Israel and Egypt, the declaration revealed the Community's desire for a greater involvement in the peace process. Indeed, the EC, by defining important issues that needed to be tackled for the peaceful settlement of the conflict, suggested "an alternative  diplomatic route on the Arab-Israel question to that forged by the United States at Camp David" (Spyer 2004: 95)

With the Venice Declaration, the EC member states expressed their conviction that the time had come for the promotion of the two principles that are accepted universally by the international community, namely; "the right to existence and to security of all the states in the region, including Israel" and "justice for all the peoples, which implies the recognition of the legitimate rights of the Palestinian people" (Art. 5). The Palestinian problem was seen as part of the Israeli-Palestinian conflict rather than as part of the Arab-Israeli conflict and. Here, in Art. 6, the Community openly stated that the refugee was an important aspect of the wider conflict:

"A just solution must finally be found to the Palestinian problem, which is not simply one of refugees. The Palestinian people, which is conscious of existing as such, must be placed in a position, by an appropriate process defined within the framework of the comprehensive peace settlement, to exercise fully its right to self-determination."

The statement went beyond previous EC declarations in that it clearly implied for the first time the recognition of the PLO as the legitimate negotiating partner in the diplomatic process. Art. 7 state that:

"The achievement of these objectives (including a just solution to Palestinian problem) requires the involvement and support of all the parties concerned in the peace settlement which the nine are endeavouring to promote in keeping with the principles formulated in the declaration referred to above. These principles apply to all the parties concerned, and thus to the Palestinian people, and to the PLO, which will have to be associated with the negotiations" (Parenthesis added).

Furthermore, the Nine once more called for the withdrawal of Israeli forces from the territories that it had maintained since the Six-Day war and announced that the Israeli settlements constituting an obstacle to the success of the peace process were illegal in international law (Art. 9). The Community also rejected any "unilateral initiative designed to change the status of Jerusalem" and stressed that "any agreement on the city's status should guarantee freedom of access for everyone to the holy places" (Art. 8). The refusal of the EC individual member states to participate in any unilateral action in the resolution of the conflict concerning Jerusalem and their reference to international law illustrate the Community's commitment to collective action, compromise, negotiation and the rule of law in international affairs.

Given that the European stance on the issue still relies on this statement, the Venice declaration is regarded by many as a milestone in the development of common EC positions towards the Middle East conflict (Hollis 1997, 18). After the adoption of this declaration, the EC intensified its efforts to increase its engagement in the political issues of the conflict through its initiation of and participation in international peace initiative. Furthermore, as Hollis indicates, "Europe's line on the Palestinians has evolved incrementally after Venice towards a more forthright endorsement of the Palestinian right to self-determination and the importance of involving the PLO in peace negotiations" (Hollis 1997, 19).

The Palestinians praised the Venice Declaration as they considered it as an important step in the right direction, even though the PLO wanted to be officially recognised by the EC as the sole representative of the Palestinian people. In total contrast, Israel furiously denounced the EC statement. The Israeli government considered even the indirect recognition of the PLO as a negotiating partner and the only representative of the Palestinians unacceptable for the reason that at that time, the Israeli forces were engaged in intense fighting with the PLO in the occupied territories. This is stressed by Spyer, who states that since "the PLO at this time was still unambiguously committed to Israel's destruction (...) the Venice Declaration was roundly criticized by Israel and the United States" (Spyer 2004, 95).

Faced with the Community's growing critical position towards its policy, and armed with the military and financial support of the United States, Israel clearly showed its willingness to pursue independent policies vis-à-vis the Community and its members. Indeed, the frustration of the Israeli government concerning the European stance on the Arab-Israeli conflict was manifested in its statement following the Venice Declaration:

> "Since Mein Kampf was written, the entire world, including Europe, has not heard anything more explicit about the aspiration to destroy the Jewish State and Nation. Several European states are prepared to underwrite, and even to guarantee militarily, the concept of "peace" shared by that organisation of murderers (...) Israel is capable of defending herself (...) Any person of goodwill or freeman who peruses this document will see it as a Munich-like surrender, the second in our generation, to dictatorial blackmail and as encouragement for all those who are subverting the Camp David accords and who aspire to ensure the failure of the Middle East Peace Plan" (Quoted in Harpaz 2005, 59).

Harpaz argues that with this statement, Israel, by explicitly rejecting the indirect two-state solution proposed by the EC in Venice declaration of 1980, demonstrated its unease with Europe's attempts to intervene in Israeli's affairs (Harpaz 2005, 59).

The US response to the Venice Declaration was more or less similar to that of the Israeli officials. In the eyes of the US government, the EC, with its special emphasis on the centrality of the Palestinian question for Middle East peace process, had partially downgraded the peace treaty that was negotiated by the US President Carter between Egypt and Israel. The American side called into question the helpfulness and effectiveness of the Community's role by arguing that the European pro-Arab policy towards the conflict is directly motivated by the Community's interests in economic gains and continuous oil supply from the region (Noor 2004, 32).

In June 1982, Israeli forces entered Lebanon in an attempt to eliminate the PLO's military threat from its northern border. An intense bombardment by Israeli army resulted in serious losses for the PLO. Moreover, with Syria's entry into war, the Syrian air defence structure was drastically destroyed, which meant for Syria another defeat in the Middle East conflict (Youngs et al. 2007).

This Israeli invasion of Lebanon was strongly condemned by the Community, who again called for the immediate withdrawal of the Israeli forces from the Lebanese territories. On 15 June 1982 at the European Parliament in Strasbourg, Mr. Tindemans, President-in-Office of the Council and Foreign Minister of Belgium, declared the European position towards the Lebanon crisis as follows:

> "Meeting in Bonn on 9 June, the Ten strongly condemned the invasion of Lebanon by the Israeli armed forces as a violation of international law, involving the danger of escalation into a general conflict (...) The Community intends to use all resources at its disposal to help to alleviate the suffering of the victims" (152).

In 1986, the Community agreed on the direct shipment of goods from the occupied territories to EC member states and gave preferential access to the Community market. This step is regarded as the "de facto recognition of the occupied territories" by the European Community (Noor 2004, 33).

In 1987, the first Palestinian 'intifada' (uprising) broke out in the occupied Palestinian territories causing more tensions and violence between the Israelis and Palestinians (Süer et al. 2006). The European answer to the Palestinian intifada came from the European Parliament, which revealed that the Community's critical position towards Israel was further fuelled by the incidents that were taking place in the occupied territories. As a response to the Israeli activities in the Palestinian territories, the Europeans decided to postpone the entry into force the three protocols signed with Israel as regards trade and financial cooperation. EC also intensified its efforts to create direct trade ties with the Palestinian and to that end EC specified conditions concerning Israeli exports originating from the occupied territories (Noor 2004, 34).

On 15 November 1988, the Palestinian National Council (PNC) in Alger proclaimed the State of Palestine with Jerusalem as its capital. Unlike the time of the first attempt of the Palestinian people to do this in Gaza during the war of

1948, this time the international community showed great interest in the Alger Declaration of 1988 (Süer et al. 2006, 76-77).

The EC reaction to PNC's proclamation came only six days after the meeting in Alger with a common statement in which the Community reemphasized its commitment to collective solutions and decisions in the resolution of international disputes:

"The Twelve attach particular importance to the decisions adopted by the Palestinian National Council in Algiers, which reflect the will of the Palestinian people to assert their national identity and which include positive steps towards the peaceful settlement of the Arab-Israeli conflict. They welcome in this respect the acceptance by the Palestinian National Council of Security Council Resolutions 242 and 338[13] as a basis for an international conference, which implies acceptance of the right of existence and of security for all states of the region, including Israel (...) For the Twelve it constitutes a necessary condition for the establishment of just, lasting and comprehensive peace in the Near East, as they have repeatedly asserted since the Declaration of Venice. The Twelve also express their satisfaction that the Palestine National Council has explicitly condemned terrorism. The Twelve appeal to all parties concerned, while abstaining from any act of violence and any action which could further aggravate the tense situation in the Near East, to take this opportunity and contribute to the peace process in a positive way with a view to a just, global and lasting solution to the Arab-Israeli conflict. This solution can only be achieved through an international peace conference under the auspices of the United Nations, which represents the suitable framework for the necessary negotiations between the parties directly concerned" (Quoted in Dehousse 1990, 378).

As illustrated in detail, in the framework of European Political Cooperation, the EC repeatedly declared its support for a just and permanent peace in the Middle East which, in its eyes, could only be achieved with the Israeli withdrawal from the occupied territories as well as with the acknowledgement of the rights of the Palestinian people. In the 1977 Declaration, the EC members

---

[13] Following the October War, The UN Security Council adopted Resolution 338, which, together with Resolution 242, became the main references in Middle East diplomatic efforts. With Resolution 338, the UN Security Council called upon all parties of the conflict to present fighting to cease all firing and terminate all military activity immediately. The Resolution also called upon all parties concerned to start after the cease-fire the implementation of Resolution 242 of 1967.

even indicated the need for establishing a Palestinian "homeland", a condition unacceptable to Israel and the U.S. at that time. Again, during the same period, the European Community, in various statements, implicitly and explicitly pointed to its preference for a comprehensive solution to the Arab-Israeli conflict rather than a bilateral approach as endorsed by Israel, the US and Egypt at Camp David.

Nevertheless, the Community's involvement in the MEPP did not go beyond declarations and remained, as in the Euro-Arab Dialogue, largely in the economic sphere: "Although all these EC statements caused considerable controversy, they did not develop into effective policies" (Leeuwen 1999, 10). The Euro-Arab Dialogue, initiated in 1973 and suspended after the Egyptian and Israeli agreement on Camp David Accords, failed to materialise. Likewise, the outcome of the GMP was not as satisfactory as expected though "it was a step forward to enhance the international role of EC and its name as the "civilian power of Europe" (Söyler quoted in Noor 2004, 28).

This more subordinate political role of the Community in the MEPP was mostly due to the diverging political and economic interests of the member states in the Mediterranean region (Renk 2005). The problems resulting from this disunity among the member states were further exacerbated by the institutional complexities of the EC foreign policy making (Youngs et al. 2007). In other words, the intergovernmental nature of the decision-making mechanism in EPC and the lack of permanent institutions in external affairs were the key impediments to the Community's attempts to develop its political presence in the peace process.

## 4.2. CFSP and the Middle East

The collapse of the Soviet Union and the fall of the Iron Curtain led to fundamental geopolitical shifts in the global security environment with new security challenges for international relations. In the Middle East, with the end of bipolarity owing to the substantial decline in Soviet power, the threat that the Arab-Israeli conflict could escalate into a superpower confrontation disappeared. Also, as a result of the significant decrease in Russian arms supply and aid to the Arab States, Moscow and Washington no longer regarded the Mediterranean as "an arena for superpower rivalry" (Youngs 2001a, 17).

However, the Iraqi invasion of Kuwait caused a radical change in regional dynamics leading to an increase in the number of players in the Gulf region. In addition, after its support for Iraq during the Gulf conflict of 1991/1992, the PLO lost the Arab financial and political backing, which it had previously enjoyed (Youngs 2001a, 17).

These security-related changes gave the conflicting parties a sense of urgency in initiating a process of direct negotiations that would involve Israel, Jordan, Lebanon, Syria and the Palestinians. Thanks to diplomatic cooperation between the US and the Soviet Union, the Madrid Conference was launched in autumn 1991 with the goal of agreeing on a comprehensive and permanent solution to the Arab-Israeli conflict. The Israeli side strongly opposed direct talks with the PLO, which it still viewed as a terrorist organisation dedicated to the destruction of the State of Israel. Hence, the Palestinian representatives took part as the member of a joint Jordanian-Palestinian delegation team with 14 delegates in total The Madrid Conference enabled Syrians, Palestinians, Jordanian, Egyptian and Israelis to conduct direct negotiations. Non-conflict parties which attended the conference were the US, the Soviet Union and the EC. In addition, the UN, the Gulf Cooperation Council and the Arab Maghreb Union participated as observers (Hollis 1997; Migdalovitz 2005).

The Madrid conference established two separate, but at the same time, parallel negotiating tracks. The multilateral track, commenced in May 1992, aimed at improving regional cooperation in five key areas of common interests; water resources, environment, arms control, refugees and economic development. In the multilateral track both conflict parties and non-conflict parties were present. The bilateral track initiated two different sets of negotiations with Israel on the one hand, and Syria, Lebanon and the joint Jordanian-Palestinian negotiating delegation on the other. In November 1991, the Israel-Palestinian track was established, the negotiations of which were based on a two-state procedure; a five-year period of interim Palestinian self-rule in the

West Bank and Gaza Strip, and negotiations on the permanent status which were to begin in the third year (Migdalovitz 2005, 3).

The EC, together with the UN, was invited as a participant to the conference, but was entirely excluded from the bilateral negotiation process. This was due mainly to the differences between the two sides of the Atlantic, the EC calling once more on Israel to end its settlement policies in the occupied territories, and accept the Palestinian land proposal. Indeed, with its adherence to a two-state solution and its repeated criticism for the Israeli policies in the region, the European Community took in the opposite direction of the US government, which was undoubtedly the main Israeli supporter at that time. Leeuwen argues that it is owing to the pro-Arab policy orientation of the EC that:

> "(…) the United States disliked the European Community's efforts at prescribing the desirable outcome of the negotiations. At various crucial stages in the negotiation process, the United States told the Community to mind its own business. It happened again during the preparations to and the follow-up of the Madrid Conference in 1991" (Leeuwen 1999, 13).

Yet, with the Madrid Conference of 1991, the EU became the coordinator of the Regional Economic Development Working Group (REDWG) which is the largest and most active working group concerning participation and the number of projects. The aim of the projects in the framework of REDWG was to organise activities and develop future projects that could contribute to the regional economic integration, and interdependence between the conflicting parties. REDWG as a whole was designed to contribute to the economic, political and humanitarian conditions of the people in the region (Peters 2004). The task of the European Union is to offer its expertise and experience concerning economic integration and support the integration process by providing financial and economic support (Asseburg 2003, 17).

In 1994, the REDWG created a monitoring centre composed of the four regional partners of the Madrid Conference; Egypt, Israel, Jordan and the Palestinians. A year later, the working group established a permanent secretariat in Amman, which is the first and still the only regional institution where the officials from the above mentioned countries work together on a daily basis (Peters 2004). Yet, as Asseburg points out, with the other multilateral working groups, the achievement of the REDWG is far from satisfactory. Asseburg argues that an ongoing and genuine peace is crucial for the progress in areas specified by the REDWG such as confidence building, regional integration and regional economic development. Nevertheless, Asseburg appreciates the Union's commitment to multilateralism by paying attention to the fact that:

> "problems which exist across borders need to be solved in multilateral frameworks that take into account the interests of all concerned parties and build on the expertise in the different sectors. It would therefore be wrong to abandon the regional and multilateral approaches" (Asseburg 2003, 17).

### 4.2.1. Oslo Accords

During 1993, bilateral negotiations between the official representatives of Israel and PLO were conducted by the mediation of the Norwegian Government. After months of secret talks in Oslo, the two sides declared in August 1993 that they had agreed on a Declaration of Principles, which came into effect on 13 October 1993 after an Israeli-Palestinian Liaison Committee was created to oversee the implementation of the principles (Youngs 2001a).

The declaration envisaged the establishment of a Palestinian self-rule in most parts of the Gaza Strip and West Bank town of Jericho, for a transitional period not exceeding five years. The Palestinian self-government was to include a Palestinian Authority based in Gaza and chaired by Arafat, as well as an elected Council with jurisdiction over Gaza and the West Bank. Besides, the Declaration acknowledged the transfer of authority over domestic affairs (with the exception of security and foreign affairs) to the Palestinian people (Süer, et al. 2006, 90-92; Youngs 2001a, 19).

The European Union welcomed the first direct PLO-Israeli government negotiations with the hope that this initiative would contribute to the settlement of a long-lasting peace in the region:

> "The reason why Europe embraced the Oslo process so enthusiastically was that Oslo in a sense offered a similar pledge: it promised to create a new Europe in the Middle East, a place where the main obstacles in the European mind to a peaceful resolution to the conflict, mainly religion and

nationalism, would finally be removed, creating a border-free common area, where peoples, once their burdensome tribal identities had been put aside, could finally come together and make peace, assisted by a substantial economic "peace dividend" that would cement peace by making a return to war simply too costly" (Ottolenghi quoted in Ottolenghi 2006, 14).

However, the European Union and even Norway, who secretly hosted the meetings, were excluded from the political part of the negotiations. Apparently, the US again wanted to restrict the role of the Europeans to economic and multilateral negotiations. This reluctance of the US to include the Europeans to the political part of the accords gave them a new impetus to become more engaged in the peace process by supporting the conflicting parties in their efforts to create an environment that would lead to a permanent peace in the region (Noor 2004, 35).

Therefore, the EU placed the financial and economic assistance at the core of its engagement with the Middle East peace process. Within the framework of Oslo, the EU and its member states became the biggest donor to the Palestinian Authority. Between 1993 and 2000, the EU countries committed a total of €1.42 billion to the development of the occupied territories which made more than 50 percent of the whole aid provided by the international community for the PA (Asseburg 2003, 12).

Asseburg argues that with financial aid and economic cooperation, the EU pursued three main objectives. First, the EU aimed to contribute to the elimination of hostilities between Palestinians and Israelis through its continuous financial and technical support for Palestinian efforts to create the necessary framework for economic growth and the well-being of the Palestinian population. Second, EU believed that the security of Israel and stability of the region could only be achieved if a democratic and viable Palestinian state with borders recognised by all the countries in the region was created. Third, EU sought to eliminate radical views and prejudices on both sides by initiating civil society projects that would enable the conflict parties to work together for common objectives (Asseburg 2003, 12).

After Oslo, large amount of aid was committed to the establishment of democratic institutions for the Palestinian self-government. Again within the framework of Oslo, the EU provided generous financial assistance for pro-jects aiming at building up the infrastructure, such as hospitals and schools, road networks, water wells and pipelines, the Gaza Harbour and airport in the Palestinian Authority. The EU also supported the Palestinians in their efforts to establish a regulatory framework for a free-market economy. Nevertheless, the intended outcome of the EU's financial and economic support for the Pal-estinian Territories was far from being satisfactory since the PA made little economic progress necessary for covering its budget without foreign support, for which the closure policies of the Israeli government was the main reason. With the introduction of closure policies by the Israeli forces, the Palestinians were not allow to enter (or work in) Israel and Jerusalem and even travel be-tween the Gaza Strip and West Bank without Israeli permission. Therefore, in the years 1992-1996, unemployment in the Palestinian territories increased by nearly 30 per cent, and consequently the per capita income decreased by almost 35 percent. Moreover, owing to the lack of the rule of law in the Pales-tinian Authority and the uncertainty about the future of the peace process, pri-vate investment failed to reach the expected level (Asseburg 2003, 13).

The joint projects for regional and bilateral Israeli-Palestinian cooperation in the fields of water, economy, trade and environment similarly failed to achieve the intended results. Asseburg offers an explanation for the unsuccessful out-come of these projects, which bears an obvious resemblance to the argu-ments made in many EU declarations: "The underlying problem is that genu-ine rapprochement and equal participation are just not possible as long as the asymmetrical, hierarchical relationship of the occupier and the occupied con-tinues to dominate people's daily lives" (Asseburg 2003, 15).

In short, at Oslo again, the Europeans were excluded from the political as-pects of the dialogue or were only allowed to participate in the multilateral ne-gotiations. Yet, as the main donor to state- and institution-building in the Pal-estinian Authority, the Union succeeded in increasing its engagement in the Middle East peace process. Furthermore, after Oslo, thanks to the Union's continuous attempts for a more active role in the pursuit of an internationally supported solution to the Arab-Israeli conflict, the EU member states of the southern Europe such as Greece and Spain gradually developed their relations with Israel, altering their traditional position towards the conflicting parties (Leeuwen 1999, 10).

### 4.2.2. The Euro-Mediterranean Partnership

The Euro-Mediterranean Partnership (Barcelona Process), a multilateral framework of political, economic and social relations between the EU and the partners of the southern Mediterranean, was launched in 1995 at the Euro-Mediterranean Conference of the Ministers of Foreign Affairs with the goal of making the Mediterranean region an "area of dialogue, exchange and cooperation guaranteeing peace, stability and prosperity." With the Barcelona Process, the EU aimed to refine its relations with the countries in the southern periphery and establish a new framework for peaceful and cooperative relations with the Mediterranean region. The partners of the Barcelona Process, other than the EU, were the Palestinian Authority, Israel, Jordan, Lebanon, Syria and Turkey, while Libya and Mauritania were invited as special guests.

The EMP is structured in three broad categories; a political and security partnership based on the principles of human rights and democracy, of dialogue and cross-cultural respect as well as on the observance of the principles of international law; an economic and financial partnership with the goal of establishing a free-trade area by 2010; and a social and cultural dialogue aiming at promoting cultural exchanges and knowledge of other languages.

The principal aim of the first part of the Barcelona Declaration was to create a "common area of peace and security" in the Mediterranean region, for which the participants decided to undertake the following principles and objectives:

> " -   to develop the rule of law and democracy in their political systems (...);
> -   respect human rights and fundamental freedoms and guarantee the effective legitimate exercise of such rights and freedoms, including freedom of expression, freedom of association for peaceful purposes and freedom of thought, conscience and religion, both individually and together with other members of the same group, without any discrimination on grounds of race, nationality, language, religion or sex; (...)

- respect and ensure respect for diversity and pluralism in their societies, promote tolerance between different groups in society and combat
  manifestations of intolerance, racism and xenophobia (...);
- respect the territorial integrity and unity of each of the other partners;
- settle their disputes by peaceful means (...);
- strengthen their cooperation in preventing and combating terrorism, in
  particular by ratifying and applying the international instruments they
  have signed, by acceding to such instruments and by taking any other
  appropriate measure;
- fight together against the expansion and diversification of organized
  crime (...)
- promote regional security by acting, inter alia, in favour of nuclear,
  chemical and biological non-proliferation through adherence to and
  compliance with a combination of international and regional non-
  proliferation regimes, and arms control and disarmament agreements
  (...) and/or regional arrangements (...) as well as by fulfilling in good
  faith their commitments under arms control, disarmament and non-
  proliferation conventions."

The second chapter of the Barcelona Declaration emphasized the significance of sustainable economic and social development for achieving the objective of establishing "an area of shared responsibility." In this context, the
partners of the EMP agreed on a closer economic and financial partnership to
achieve their objective of creating a free-trade area by 2010- Partners also
agreed on closer cooperation in relevant areas such as technology, environment, agriculture and investment and EU member states declared their willingness to provide economic support for the Mediterranean countries. The
driving force behind the Union's efforts to promote economic development
amongst its southern neighbours "was the belief that the root causes of instability in the Mediterranean region were economic underdevelopment and social inequality and that these issues needed to be tackled collectively within a
multilateral framework" (Peters 2004, 3).

The third and last chapter of the EMP aimed to establish a partnership in social, cultural and human affairs, which the EU describes as a crucial element
"in bringing the people closer, promoting understanding between societies
and improving their perception of each other." The participants also expressed their determination to combat racism, xenophobia and intolerance in

their attempts to encourage cross-cultural exchanges among the peoples of the EU and the Mediterranean region.

The Euro-Mediterranean Partnership is based on three aspects: First, there is a multilateral dimension which includes all participants of the Barcelona Process and encompasses the topics covered within the framework of the Association Agreements. Partners are represented by their foreign ministers, including the Palestinian Authority. The representatives of the EU are individual member states and the Commission as the only supranational body of the EU. Second, there is a bilateral dimension based on the same logic as the GMP. The bilateral dimensions involve meeting between the EU and individual Mediterranean countries. Third, there is a unilateral dimension with the Union acting as the only decision-making partner. The three dimensions might seem separate, however, "all the three of them state region building as their purpose, and they all address the multifaceted EMP agenda. The multilateral and the bilateral dimension are articulated at various levels of the diplomatic hierarchy, ranging from the highest, ministerial level to the level of working groups" (Bicchi 2004: 7).

The financial and technical support for the implementation of the EMP is provided by the MEDA programme implemented by the Commission's Directorate General (DG) EuropAid Cooperation Office which is responsible for preparing the annual financial plans and implementing external aid instruments of the European Commission. The Council Decision 96/706/EC on MEDA programme sets out a roadmap for the Union's support for the reform efforts in the Mediterranean region. The member states summarizes the objective of the MEDA programme as follows: "The programme has the main purpose of encouraging and supporting the reform of the economic and social structures of the Mediterranean partners, notably in preparation for free trade with the European Community." (Annex 1).To that end, EU decided to provide economic assistance to its southern neighbours in order to "help to prepare (the Mediterranean) for free trade with the Community and to raise the standard of living. The wider objective of Community interventions will be to increase the competitiveness of the partners' economies, with a view to achieving sustainable economic growth, in particular through improved export performance."

(Annex 15). The financial instruments are also applied in order to enhance the socio-economic balance with the aim of lessening the negative aspects of economic transition.

Although the Barcelona Declaration affirms "the principle of separateness" between the Barcelona Process and the Israeli-Palestinian conflict (Moschella 2004: 11) by pointing out that "Euro-Mediterranean initiative is not intended to replace the other activities and initiatives undertaken in the interests of the peace, stability and development of the region, but that it will contribute to their success", there is a reciprocal relationship between them. In other words, the EMP was:

> "(...) designed to be complementary to the Middle East peace process by providing a framework through which, among partners, parties to the conflict would be able to build up trust and institutionalise their relations in their po- litical, economic and human spheres as well as in the field of security. It was supposed to serve the aim of peace-building and long-term regional stabili- sation by laying foundations for economic development and regional integra- tion" (Asseburg 2003, 16).

One of the greatest achievements of the Barcelona Process with regard to the Middle East peace process was to attribute to the Palestinian Authority the status of an equal Mediterranean partner recognised by all other partici- pants (Moschella 2004: 11). In addition, the EMP, by providing all the coun- tries involved in the conflict with a regular forum for dialogue, played a signifi- cant role in the Arab States' acceptance of Israel as a partner in the process of peace settlement. The Union's decision to include Israel in Barcelona Process:

> "(...) was based on the assumption that a fundamental change in Israeli- Arab relations had occurred, and that the Arab states of the Euro- Mediterranean partnership were now prepared to accept Israel as an equal and legitimate partner and that they would be willing to engage with Israel in a new set of multilateral ventures at the regional level" (Peters 2004, 4-5).

However, Israeli military presence in Lebanon and the use of violence in the occupied territories presented obstacles to the peace process. With the out- break of the second intifada, Syria and Lebanon boycotted Marseilles (2000) and Valencia (2002) Ministerial Conferences as a protest against the Israeli reaction to Palestinian uprising (Moschella 63-64).Therefore, the EMP "has not been able to stop violence nor to develop confidence among the parties involved in the conflict" (Peters 2004: 11).

Supporters of the Euro-Mediterranean Partnership pay attention to the developments made after the launch of the Barcelona Process in 1995 such as the signing of Association agreements, the increase in trade flows among the partner countries, the progress accomplished within the framework of political dialogue and the establishment of several networks connecting the civil society. Nevertheless, the partnership has failed the remove the economic gap between the EU member states and the Mediterranean region. Despite the significant progress in bilateral economic relations between the European Union and many of the Southern Mediterranean partners, the objective of establishing new cooperative structures in the Mediterranean region to achieve sustainable economic growth failed to bring concrete results. Obviously, very little progress has been made in eradicating the prejudices and misperceptions or in strengthening cross-cultural dialogue among the societies in the region. In the absence of a political settlement of the Arab-Israeli conflict and in the presence of a huge imbalance of economic and military power between Israel and the Arab states, no confidence has been built between the partners (Asseburg 2003, 16).

These regional obstacles have combined with the EU inability to tackle regional disputes such as the second intifada and the Israeli occupation of the Lebanese territory. Many analysts, however, argue that the real problem within the Barcelona Process has been the gap between the rhetoric and the actual policy implementation of the European Union. Indeed, in cases of human rights violations by both sides or the Palestinian failure in democratic reforms, the member states demonstrated a lack of political unity when it came to applying economic sanctions to individual Mediterranean countries. The impotence caused by the inability of the EU to act with unity and decisiveness in applying sanctions has become more evident in its relations with Israel and the Palestinian Authority. Here, the Union failed to set an embargo on arms selling to Israel or revise the Israeli preferential agreement with the European Union. In the same way, the member states seemed to be reluctant to apply economic sanctions against the Palestinian Authority as a response to human rights abuses and lack of transparency in political institutions (Tanner 2002, 6; Attinà 2003, 191).

In an overall assessment of the EMP, Attinà highlights the various internal constraints in EU foreign policy cooperation, all of which hamper the Union's ability to implement its intended Middle East strategy:

> "In general, some member countries (usually former colonial powers) para-
> lyse the application of sanctions for the special relations existing with the po-
> tential target state and the desire to preserve their own "reserved domain"
> from interference from other EU countries" (Attinà 2003, 191).

In October 1996 the EU, for the first time, appointed a special envoy to the Middle East peace process, the Spanish diplomat Miguel Moratinos, whose assignment was to maintain close contacts with the conflicting parties as well as with key regional and international players involved in the peace process. His mandate also included participating in negotiations, offering suggestions for the implementation of international agreements when required and promoting the fundamental principles of democracy. One of the Moratinos' most important achievements regarding the Arab-Israeli conflict was his participation in Taba Talks between the Israelis and the Palestinians in 2001 where he was asked by both parties to listen to their individual standpoints in the conflict after which he prepared a full summary of discussions made at the negotiation table (Dannreuther 2002, 10-14).

The period of 1998-2000 is regarded by many as the most productive period of EU involvement in the Middle East peace process. Indeed, with the appointment of Javier Solana to the post of High Representative of the Common Foreign and Security Policy in 1999, the EU can be definitely said to have achieved an even stronger presence in the region. As the representative of the European Union, Solana was directly involved in the Sharm-el-Sheik negotiations of 2000, the Mitchell Commission, and the Quartet diplomacy of 2003 (Asseburg 2003, 18). Therefore, as Dannreuther (2002: 9) concludes, "the appointment in 1999 of the former Secretary General of NATO, Javier Solana, to the post of High Representative of the CFSP, provided enhanced political credibility and offered a much-needed element of continuity to EU policy which could buttress the work of Moratinos."

Again in 1999, after several tough efforts to come to a common position, the EU member states issued their most explicit common statement in support of a Palestinian state. With the Berlin Declaration of 1999:

> "The European Union reaffirms the continuing and unqualified Palestinian right to self-determination including the option of a state and looks forward to the early fulfillment of this right (...) The European Union is convinced that the creation of a democratic, viable and peaceful sovereign Palestinian State on the basis of existing agreements and through negotiations would be the best guarantee of Israel's security and Israel's acceptance as an equal partner in the region. The European Union declares its readiness to consider the recognition of a Palestinian State in due course in accordance with the basic principles referred to above."

Although the declaration openly stated the Union's support for an independent Palestinian state whose existence would also ensure the future security of Israel in the region it was a diplomatic attempt on the EU side, in coordination with the US, to prevent a unilateral declaration of the State of Palestine by Arafat (Dannreuther 2002, 10).

On 1 April 2000, Chris Patten, the EU's Commissioner for External Relations, paid an official visit to Egypt. Four days later, during his first trip to Israel as the Commissioner of EU External Relations, he gave a speech wherein he reiterated the Union's willingness to enhance its relations with its neighbours in the southern Mediterranean as well as its commitment to the fundamental principles of Barcelona Declaration of 1995 and the Euro-Mediterranean Partnership.

Furthermore, in June 2000, the European Union adopted a common strategy on the Mediterranean region in which the member states reemphasised their conviction that the success of the Middle East peace process was a pivotal factor for the creation of a "prosperous, democratic, stable and secure region, with an open perspective towards Europe" (Part 1. 1.) With regard to the resolution of the Arab-Israeli conflict, the EU decided to:

> - provide its expertise, submit ideas and make available its good offices and  assistance to the core parties of the Peace Process in order to facili-

tate the conclusion of peace agreements and help prepare the 'post peace era' in the Middle East,

- actively promote progress on the multilateral track of the Peace Process drawing also on synergies with the Barcelona Process. With regard to central issues such as water and refugees, the EU will offer its expertise whenever requested,
- in the context of a comprehensive settlement, and on request by the core parties, give consideration to the participation of Member States in the implementation of security arrangements on the ground,
- contribute to the international commitment needed to implement and con-solidate peace in the Middle East, notably through support to regional economic cooperation and integration and the expansion of trade flows.
- work towards strengthening stability in the Middle East by means of coop-erative security through its contributions to the implementation of the Eu-ro-Mediterranean Charter for Peace and Stability once it is adopted and has entered into force" (Part 1. 15).

The adoption of the common strategy on the Mediterranean is a positive de-velopment of a European policy towards the Middle East for two main rea-sons. First, it was the third common strategy adopted after those of Russia and Ukraine. Therefore, EU reemphasized how important the Mediterranean region is for the Union's strategic, economic and political priorities. Second, thanks to the extension of the scope of QMV, it became possible to imple-ment the strategy through common positions and joint actions, though this has so far failed to materialize.

### 4.2.3.  Second Intifada and post- 9/11

Because of the continuing disagreements between the Israelis and the Pales-tinians, especially over the territory of the future Palestinian state as well as the status of Jerusalem, the five-year period of the Israel-PLO agreement ex-pired in 1998 without any concrete outcome. In addition, the Sharm-al-Sheik negotiations, initiated with the objective of reaching a permanent status agreement and ending violence at both sides, had achieved very little. Under these circumstances, the newly elected Israeli Prime Minister Ehud Barak and the President of the Palestinian Authority attended a summit at Camp David in summer 2000 (Youngs 2001b).

As Youngs points out in his research paper *The Middle East Crisis: Camp David, the 'Al-Aqsa Intifada' and the Prospects for the Peace Process*, the main goal of the Camp David negotiations was to resolve the final status of the most critical issues of the Middle East conflict, such as the status of Jerusalem, Palestinian refugees, natural resources as well as territory, borders and the Jewish settlements However, apart from declaring their determination to conclude an agreement on the above mentioned issues as soon as possible, and agreeing to oppose any kind of unilateral action that could endanger the peace process, Barak and Arafat left the Camp David negotiations without a final agreement and without practical proposals for the resolution of the disputes. In addition, as in the first Camp David meeting in 1979, the EU was not regarded as a partner, because of the bilateral nature of the negotiation process (Youngs 2001b, 9-20).

In October 2000, the second intifada (Al-Aqsa Intifada) of the Palestinians broke out. The main reason behind the intifada was undoubtedly the decades of peace negotiations without tangible outcome. However, violence intensified as Ariel Sharon, the leader of the conservation Likud party in Israel, paid a visit to Haram Al-Sharif in Jerusalem. Haram al-Sharif was one of the issues over which Palestinians and Israelis had not reached a final agreement. Therefore, Palestinians responded to Sharon's visit through demonstrations, which, however, led to eruption of violence all around Israel and the PA causing many deaths on the Palestinian side. After a few weeks, the number of Palestinians demonstrating against Sharon increased rapidly leading to more unrest in the region (Youngs 2001b, 25-26)

> "The demonstrations came as a shock to the Israeli establishment and drew attention to the growing frustrations among Israeli Arabs at perceived routine discrimination against them within Israeli society. The clashes prompted warnings from some observers that prolonged violence in the territories and a failure to address the inequalities between Israeli Arabs and Jews could lead to a further radicalisation of the Israeli Arab population." (Youngs 2001b: 26).

Unlike the US government, the EU held Sharon's visit to the Temple Mount responsible for the outburst of violence (Noor 2004, 37). In 2001, in the report of the Sharm el-Sheik Fact-Finding Committee, the Committee members, including the High Representative of CFSP, Javier Solana, concluded that, though not the real cause, the Sharon visit "was poorly timed and the provocative effect should have been foreseen; indeed it was foreseen by those who urged that the visit be prohibited" (13).

During October and November, a number of talks took place with the goal of putting an end to the violent attacks and initiating a new peace process period. As a result of Palestinian call for the participation of other regional and international actors in the talks, a number of actors, including President Clinton, UN Secretary-General Kofi Annan, the EU High Representative Javier Solana, King Abdullah of Jordan and President Mubarak of Egypt were invited to the Sharm-el Sheik Summit between Barak and Arafat. A key decision at the negotiations was the agreement by both sides on the creation of an international investigation tem with the CFSP representative, Javier Solana as one of the investigators (Youngs 2001b, 31-32).

Fear of a further escalation of bloody incidents in the West Bank and the Gaza Strip led to the launch of Taba negotiations in January 2001. Nevertheless, due to the political disorder in Israel (according to the public polls, Barak was about to be replaced by a new prime minister) as well as Palestinian dissatisfaction with the final offer made by the Israeli side, the Taba talks failed to reach a commonly accepted solution. Yet, in terms of the Union's involvement in the Middle East peace process, the Taba talks are significant in the sense that it "was the first time Javier Solana succeeded in playing an influential role on behalf of the EU (...) Taba established Solana as a player" (Everts 2003: 20).

Again in the same period, through a number of declarations, the EU member states repeatedly expressed their concern about the use of violence, the suffering of the civilian population, and the hatred between the peoples of the region. At the Nice European Council Meeting in December 2000, the Union stated that a future solution to the conflict would entail the following elements:

"- the personal commitment of the Israeli Prime Minister and the President of the Palestinian Authority;

- full and immediate compliance with the undertakings which they entered into at Sharm el-Sheikh and Gaza;
- concrete gestures by both parties, with respect, inter alia, to the renunciation of violence and, as regards Israel, the settlements issue;
- the establishment of a mechanism for confidence-building measures;
- the commencement of work on the spot by the Fact-Finding Commission, in which Mr. Solana, Secretary-General/High Representative for the CFSP, will take part; an agreement on the setting up of an observer mission."

In December 2000, Israel imposed a closure of the occupied territories, prohibiting, for a few months, the Palestinian population from entering Israel as well as from travelling between the West Bank and Gaza Strip. The Israeli forces allowed a limited number of workers residing in the occupied territories to return to work in Israel but with severe restrictions and many entry permits of Palestinians were cancelled. In addition, through various obstacles such as checkpoints and iron gates, Palestinian access to main roads was blocked by the Israeli side.

These broad restrictions on the freedom of movement imposed by Israel after the outbreak of the Al-Aqsa intifada caused deterioration in the economy of the occupied territories, leading to an unprecedented increase in unemployment rates and poverty among the Palestinian population, and to a serious decrease in import and export trade (Asseburg 2003). According to a report published by the World Bank in 2002, as a result of this economic crisis Palestinian exports declined by 45 percent in value while imports contracted by a third between June 2000 and June 2002. Using a poverty line of $2 per day, the World Bank estimated that, in comparison with the pro-intifada period, the number of poor increased to about 60 per cent by December 2002, from 637,000 to just under 2 million. (1-3)

Under these circumstances, at the Stockholm European Council of March 2001, the EU called on the Israeli government to "lift closures and pay overdue revenues and the Palestinian Authority must adopt without delay an austerity budget and take effective measures against corruption and towards more democratic transparency." Similarly, at the Plenary Session of the

European Parliament in May 2001, Chris Patten referred to the negative impact of the closures and settlement policies on the Palestinian economy and drew attention to the institutional and financial collapse in the occupied territories. At that time:

> "(...) it had become obvious that sustainable economic development was not possible in the face of Israeli closure policies and the fragmentation of the Palestinian territories through the ongoing process of settlement and bypass road construction. Economic losses due to the closures have by far outweighed the international donors' disbursements to the Palestinian areas" (Asseburg 2003, 15).

Patten also raised the question of the destruction of property, particularly Arab lands and shelters in the refugee camps and properties financed by the EU. The damage to EU-funded projects either destroyed or damaged by the Israeli forces since 2002 is estimated to exceed €25 million. Nevertheless, the international community failed to impose any diplomatic penalties as a response to the Israeli demolition of Palestinian homes and property, let alone its main trading partner – the EU. This failure is surprising given that the EU was the main donor to Palestinian state-building process (Sayigh 2004, 11-12).

The EU reluctance to impose diplomatic or economic sanctions on either Israel or the Palestinian Authority results primarily from the diverging relations of EU member states with the conflicting parties as well as their different foreign policy priorities. The disunity within the EU combines with the institutional constraints of the CFSP and the consensual nature of the decision-making mechanism which, jointly, hinder the adoption of common positions towards an external dispute. For instance, when the European Parliament adopted a resolution in April 2002 calling for the suspension of the EU-Israeli Association Agreement in response to the Israeli human rights violations during the military operations in the occupied territories, there was strong disagreement within the EU over any possible application of sanctions against Israel. Whereas some member states, most explicitly Belgium, gave considerable support to the implementation of the EP resolution, France, together with others, declared its conviction that economic sanctions would not exert political pressure on Israel.

Likewise, the German government, whose criticism of Israel was extremely moderate, expressed its opposition to the suspension of the EU-Israeli Association Agreement. Therefore, Germany either chose to decline or to abstain from UN resolutions in topics, such as Israeli activities against international legal principles as well as the establishment of Israeli settlements in Palestinian territories. The UK also took a moderate attitude towards Israel (Müller 2006, 7-16).

Once again upon the construction of the "security barrier" by Israel inside the West Bank, the member states failed to agree on a joint EU diplomatic response and tried to find a multilateral approach to the problem:

> "(...) certain European states opposed taking the issue to the International Court of Justice for adjudication at Palestinian request, although all member states subsequently supported a UN General Assembly vote in line with the Court's ruling that the construction of the security fence inside the Occupied Territories was illegal and should be removed" (Sayigh 2004, 11).

In addition to a number of declarations, the EU member states provided significant financial help to eliminate the negative consequences of destruction in Palestinian Authority following the second intifada. In the mean time, the EU asserted its conviction political and economic reforms would facilitate a future peace settlement. Therefore, the EU made available substantial aid to the Palestinian state- and institution-building efforts (Noor 2004). According to the European Neighbourhood Policy (ENP) Strategy Paper published in 2004, the EU committed 277.8 million dollars from the beginning of 2000 till the end of 2003 (30). The main objective of EU financial aid was to cover the daily budgetary expenses of the PA, such as wages, education and health. The EU reiterated that progress in reforms and the existence of well-functioning democratic and transparent institutions were the basic conditions for the continuation of the overall EU financial support to the Palestinians (Asseburg 2003).

Meanwhile, the terrorist attacks of September 2001 hit the US leading to a new era for Middle Eastern politics which drastically undermined security in the Mediterranean neighbourhood. At the extraordinary European Council Meeting on 21 September 2001, the EC called for "an in-depth political dialogue with those countries and regions of the world in which terrorism comes into being' as well as 'the integration of all countries into a fair world system of security, prosperity and improved development." Furthermore, the member states expressed their willingness to play a greater role in preventing and stabilising regional conflicts, which the EU regarded as a key requirement fighting against terrorism. In terms of the Middle East, the Community invited not only the conflicting parties but also other actors such as the US and Russia to work in close collaboration for a resolution of the conflict. (3)

However, despite the fact that both the EU and the US recognised the difficulty of the challenge posed by global terrorism, the attacks of September 2001 exacerbated the already existing gap between the transatlantic partners as regards how to deal with security threats:

> "(...) it became clear that most Americans viewed terrorism as a far more urgent danger than did most Europeans, especially before the Madrid attacks in March 2004. The U.S. government was also much more willing to consider a military response as effective, while European leaders gave more emphasis to addressing the socio-economic roots of terrorism" (Aaron et al. 2004, 2).

Also, regarding their approach to dealing with regional or international conflicts, the transatlantic partners continued to express diverging views. In contrast to the US, the Union is more inclined to multilateral arrangements based on international law and soft power instruments such as diplomatic tools and foreign aid. Indeed, following the September attacks in the US, the EU member states repeatedly stressed the effectiveness of multilateralism and international cooperation in the resolution of international disputes.

For instance, at the Barcelona European Council of 15-16 March 2002, the Community repeated its support for the development of multilateral arrangements and the implementation of international decisions for the stabilisation of the conflict. With the Declaration on the Middle East, the member states declared that:

> "The European Union is determined to play its role together with the parties, the countries in the region, the US, the UN and Russia in the pursuit of a so-

lution, based on UNSC Resolutions 242, 338 and 1397[14] and on the principles of the Madrid Conference, Oslo and subsequent agreements, which would allow two states, Israel and Palestine, to live in peace and security and play their full part in the region. The High Representative, Javier Solana, will continue his regular consultations with all international actors involved" (29).

Likewise, at the Seville European Council on 21-22 June 2002, the Union reiterated its determination to cooperate with the parties and its partners in the international community, particularly within the framework of the Quartet. More significant, however, is that with the Seville Declaration on the Middle East, the member states put forward an explicit approach to the settlement of peace in the region, which in the Union's view, can be achieved only through negotiation:

> "The objective is an end to the occupation and the early establishment of a democratic, viable, peaceful and sovereign State of Palestine, on the basis of the 1967 borders, if necessary with minor adjustments agreed by the parties. The end result should be two States living side by side within secure and recognised borders enjoying normal relations with their neighbours. In this context, a fair solution should be found to the complex issue of Jerusalem, and a just, viable and agreed solution to the problem of the Palestinian refugees" (35).

The idea of an independent Palestinian state, in fact, had already been proposed by the French foreign minister, Hubert Védrine, whose peace plan of February 2002 called for the declaration of the State of Palestine as the starting point for the resumption of peace negotiations. Similarly, the German initiative known as the "Fischer plan" or "the Fischer idea", proposed that the conflict parties come together to specify the measures necessary for a long-standing peace settlement in the region. As the French idea, the German plan also called for the declaration of a Palestinian state, which would ensure the security and stability of all countries in the Middle East. Fischer plan also pro-

---

[14] Resolution 1397, adopted by the UN Security Council on 12 March 2002, recalled previous resolutions and stressed the need to respect universally accepted norms of international humanitarian law. The Security Council also welcomed the diplomatic efforts of special envoys from the United States of America, the Russian Federation, The European Union and the UN Special Coordinator. For the whole text of the resolution see Annex I.

posed greater involvement of international institutions in future peace initiatives. Moreover, Denmark presented EU member states a draft proposal and defined 2005 as the year by which an independent Palestinian state would be created. Danish peace initiative also suggested the incorporation of multilateral instruments into the peace process (Müller 2006, 9-11).

### 4.2.4. The Roadmap

Meanwhile, due to the growing scepticism among the Palestinians about the success and sincerity of the US as a mediator, the US administration intensified its efforts to involve the European Union as well as the UN and Russia in the Middle East peace process. Moreover, the US was aware that in the absence of the US, the EU would not be an efficient and coherent actor in the region. However, it was also evident that with its political and financial aid to the peace process, the EU is a more reliable partner for Palestinians than the US (Dannreuther 2002, 10). This shift in US position towards the peace settlement resulted primarily from the US observation that there was also unrest within the international community concerning the growing US unilateralism international community (Noor 2002).

Therefore, on 24 June 2002, the US President presented the idea of the Roadmap which set a comprehensive and intertwined agenda of conditions and steps that would put an end to the Palestinian-Israeli conflict, stop the violence on both sides and bring about a peace settlement. The implementation of this approach was designed as a coordinated and joint "Quartet"[15] work and was presented in late April 2003 by representatives of the Middle East Quartet to the parties of the conflict.

The so-called Roadmap, as Quartet members call it, "is a performance-based and goal-driven roadmap, with clear phases, timelines, target dates, and benchmarks aiming at progress through reciprocal steps by the two parties in

[15] Quartet, including USA, EU, UN and the Russian Federation was formally established in the fall of 2001 with the aim of collectively developing a more comprehensive strategy towards the Palestinian-Israeli conflict.

the political, security, economic, humanitarian, and institution-building fields, under the auspices of the Quartet." It envisions "a final and comprehensive settlement of the Israeli-Palestinian conflict by 2005" through a two-state solution that would be achieved in three main stages.

The role of the Quartet representatives, in this context, would be to monitor the process and provide support for the implementation of the Roadmap objectives. The Quartet would also assist the measures undertaken by the conflicting parties and to facilitate the implementation of the plan, including direct negotiations between the Israelis and Palestinians when required. Also, entry into next phases of the process depends on the unanimous evaluation of the Quartet representatives of whether the parties have successfully fulfilled the requirements of the previous phase and created the necessary conditions to advance.

The first phase of the Roadmap, which was to be completed till May 2003, concentrated on "normalization of Palestinian life and institution-building (...) ratification of a democratic Palestinian constitution, formal establishment of office of prime minister, consolidation of political reform, and the creation of a Palestinian state with provisional borders." The first step towards a permanent peace settlement is to respect the right of the other party to exist in peace and security, end in official statements the use of expressions entailing the incitement of the other party. Regarding security-related issues, the Palestinian Authority security apparatus should undertake practical efforts to tackle individuals and groups engaged in terror and fight against terrorist networks. The Israelis should also cease deportation of Palestinians, attacks on civilians, destruction of Palestinian infrastructure and property. A remarkable feature of the security aspect of the process is the active role played by the Quartet members, including the EU, in monitoring and consulting on the creation of a formal monitoring mechanism and its implementation.

On its way towards an independent, viable and democratic state, the Palestinian Authority was required to initiate a comprehensive reform process and make credible progress in preparation for statehood. The reform process should include the preparation of a draft constitution based on parliamentary democracy, the appointment of an interim prime minister with executive authority as well as ministers and the establishment of an independent Palestinian election Committee for free, fair and open elections. At this point, the Israeli side should facilitate the travel of Palestinian officials, internationally supervised security retraining as well as electoral and other reform activities. Given that the EU was the main donor to the PA at that time, the Roadmap assigned the EU an important task.

As already noted, the second phase, foreseen for the period of June 2003 and December 2004, was to begin after the unanimous decision of the Quartet members on the performance made in the previous period and after the Palestinian elections. In this phase, both parties concentrate their efforts on the creation of a Palestinian state with provisional borders and national sovereignty, living in peace and security with Israel and other neighbours in the region. Quartet members reiterated their conviction that "this goal (establishment of a Palestinian state) can be achieved when the Palestinian people have a leadership acting decisively against terror, willing and able to build a practicing democracy based on tolerance and liberty. With such a leadership, reformed civil institutions and security structures, the Palestinians will have the active support of the Quartet and the broader international community." The Roadmap foresaw an international conference organised by the Quartet after the conclusion of the Palestinian election to support the economic recovery programme of the PA. In addition, the representatives of the Quartet were expected to work for the international recognition of the Palestinian State, including its possible UN membership.

In the third and the last phase of the Roadmap, efforts are focussed on the "consolidation of reform and stabilisation of Palestinian institutions." Other objectives mentioned by the Quartet were "the sustained, effective Palestinian security performance, and Israeli-Palestinian negotiations aimed at a permanent status agreement in 2005." The third phase also envisaged an international conference aimed at agreeing on "a final, permanent status resolution in 2005, including on borders, Jerusalem, refugees, settlements." Here again, the Quartet members were to actively support the progress towards a permanent peace settlement.

The Roadmap, constituting the first joint US-EU cooperation to form a peace plan, is undoubtedly the most comprehensive and most multilateral effort thus far, aiming to end the intensified conflict since the outbreak of the second intifada in September 2000. Its diplomatic significance lies in the fact that the Roadmap document is the product of intense negotiations between the US and the three other members of the Quartet, including the EU and provides the partners with a multilateral framework for further negotiations.

The release of the Roadmap is a crucial moment in transatlantic relations, because the EU and the US, despite the disparities in their stances on various issues as regards the Middle East conflict, have been successful in bringing their individual positions for a collective response. In other words, since the establishment of the Middle East Quartet and the publication of the Roadmap text:

> "The United States and Europe have never before coordinated so closely on the Middle East peace process (...) The Europeans have finally obtained a political, not just economic, place at the peace process table while the gap appears to be narrowing between the two sides' visions of a final settlement to the Arab-Israeli conflict. Both sides have moved closer to the other's positions: the United States now supports a peace outcome (a two-state solution), not just a peace process (...) while Europe has actively moved toward U.S. positions on Palestinian reform (Kaye 2003: 183).

Moreover, the Roadmap can be seen as a diplomatic victory for the Europeans since the Union, as an essential partner of the Quartet, has gained acceptance from both the conflicting parties and the US as a significant third party in the peace process. In fact, thanks to the Union's diplomatic activities prior to the Bush statement of June 2002, the EU member states not only formulated a common position to the conflict, but they also made it clear to the US how important it was to act collectively without exclusion of regional players such as the Palestinian leader Arafat (Asseburg 2003, 24). In other words, "through the Road Map, which is the most comprehensive and most multilateral effort to date for putting an end to the deadly conflict in the Middle East, the EU has been acknowledged as an essential partner carrying its authorship rights" (Noor 2004: 43).

Nevertheless, the EU appeared powerless as the Israeli Prime Minister Ariel Sharon declared the Israeli plan of a unilateral disengagement from Gaza and from a small number of West Bank settlements. The EU, striving to preserve the multilateral aspect of the internationally supported Roadmap, expressed its scepticism and concern about the unilateral Israeli initiative which, in the eyes of the EU, could damage the intended outcome of the peace process. However, due to the strong US backing for Israel, the member states accepted the decision, yet did their utmost to "link the disengagement plan to the road map process" (Müller 2006, 15).

Indeed, at the Brussels European Council of 25 and 26 March 2004, the EU stated its position towards the Israeli initiative as follows:

"The European Council noted the proposals for an Israeli withdrawal from the Gaza Strip. Such a withdrawal could represent a significant step towards the implementation of the Roadmap, provided that, in accordance with the deliberations of the Council of 23 February:
  - it took place in the context of the Roadmap;
  - it was a step towards a two-State solution;
  - it did not involve a transfer of settlement activity to the West Bank;
  - there was an organised and negotiated handover of responsibility to the Palestinian Authority;
  - and Israel facilitated the rehabilitation and reconstruction of Gaza" (16).

Besides, the continuing disunity among the EU member states over a number of issues with regard to the Middle East conflict still remains the main obstacle to the development of the Union's involvement in the region and to a more definite European policy towards the peace process. This again occurred as the member states profoundly divided over how to react over the Hamas election victory of January 2006.

Moreover, other informal initiatives undertaken by individual member states such as the joint Spanish-French-Italian peace plan of November 2006 explicitly revealed that the member states still tend to pursue their national policies. The Spanish Prime Minister explained the motivation hidden behind this initiative as the joint Spanish-French-Italian "responsibility (...) as three Mediterranean powers" towards the Mediterranean region. Yet, this individual attempt failed to exercise any substantial influence over the parties and highlighted the importance of speaking as a single voice for the development of an effective and coherent role of the EU in the peace process as well as for the successful implementation of the Roadmap objectives (Biscop 2007, 18).

For all the reasons mentioned above, the future role of the EU in the Middle East peace process depends principally on the removal of internal constraints within the CSFP pillar and on the development of a unified stance on several issues over which the member states still have diverging views. Indeed, despite its unquestionable success in developing its economic involvement with peace negotiations, the EU has been unable to exercise any substantial political influence over the peace process (Noor 2004; Renk 2005). This political impotence is described by Noor as something that comes from the block itself:

> "The major hindrance, or say weakness comes from the bloc itself. The lack of coherence on foreign policy matters has hampered the EU from adopting concrete and consistent policies for a long time. Regarding the Middle East, some of its member states support an active and enhanced role while others prefer keeping a low profile, mostly as a move not to act in chagrin of the US which continues to enjoy the status of the sole superpower" (Noor 2004, 44).

The lack of consistency among the member states due to their historical and economic ties with the conflicting parties is exacerbated with the consensual nature of decision-making in the CFSP, different interlocutors and the rotating presidency, which all limit the Union's ability to make effective decisions within a short period of time, particularly during international crises such as the Middle East conflict. The obligation to unanimity with regard to external policy making is a major impediment to the Union's capacity to bundle its power resources for rapid reactions and apply them for a collective response, as it was the case when the member states fail to impose any sanctions either on the PA or on Israel. Therefore, it is correct to predict that in the future, the enhancement of the political presence of the EU in the Middle East region could be once more constrained by structural weaknesses within the Union, including its own disunity in foreign policy interests and the lack of effective CFSP instruments (Nonneman 2003, 45).

These institutional insufficiencies within the CFSP are reflected in its inclination towards an economic rather than a political engagement. Since the launch of its Middle East Policy, the EU has continuously sought to strengthen its economic ties with the countries involved in the conflict and provided, at the same time, tremendous financial aid to the region with the aim of creating conditions for peace, stability and prosperity in its immediate neighbourhood. In fact over the years, through a number of institution-building programmes and emergency assistance, the EU has achieved the role of prominent economic actor and become a vital financial contributor to the Middle East peace process.

In his explanation of the EU's divergent levels of success in economic and political areas, Dannreuther indicates the division between, on the other hand, the foreign and security policy which operates within the intergovernmental framework of the CFSP pillar and, on the other hand, the Union's external economic relations which works within the supranational decision-making apparatus of the European Community. In other words, the success of the EU's economic presence, both as a trading partner and as an investor in the Middle East, depends on its ability to take decisions concerning the Union's economic relations as well as financial aid to third parties at the supranational Community level.

## 5. EU-Palestinian Authority

Europe's long and complicated historical ties with the Middle East have always been the decisive factor for its position towards the conflicting parties. Especially as a result of ancient religious crusades and the colonial experiences of some European powers such as France and the Great Britain in the Arab World during the nineteenth and twentieth centuries the EU has done its utmost to preserve its strategically significant position in the region. Furthermore, as some analysts argue, the European continent feels historically and morally responsible for the creation of the state Israel and the emergence of the Palestinian question (Archick 2005, 3).

As a consequence, the EU member states have repeatedly declared their commitment to the improvement of the humanitarian and economic situation of the Palestinian people as well as their support for the establishment of institutions for the creation of a democratic, independent and viable Palestinian state living in peace and security with its neighbour Israel. The key instruments the Union applies to achieve these objectives are the Interim Association Agreement on Trade and Cooperation adopted following the establishment of the Palestinian Authority in 1996, the EU-PA European Policy Action Plan of 2005, and the Commission's financial assistance programme. In addition, the EU gives considerable support to the Palestinian reform efforts not only through its financial assistance package to the PA, but through its direct participation in the Quartet as well.

### 5.1. EC financial assistance programmes[16]

The EU is the largest donor to the Palestinian Authority. With its financial assistance programmes, the Union aims at promoting political and economic stability so as to improve the living conditions of the population in the occupied territories, and it supports at the same time the institutional reform proc-

---

[16] This part of the study rests heavily upon the information released by the European Commission Technical Office for the West Bank and Gaza, available at: <http://www.delwbg.cec.eu.int/>

ess which the Union considers vital for the establishment of a Palestinian state living in peace with Israel.

Since 1971, the EC financial assistance to the Palestinians in the fields of operation, primary health and education has been channelled through the United Nations Works and Relief Agency for Palestine Refugees in the Near East (UNWRA). According to the joint UNWRA and European Commission Report (2007) on the *EC support to UNWRA*, over the past four years, the European Commission has contributed € 246 million to UNWRA's General Fund, becoming the second largest donor after the United States of America, and plans to further contribute at least € 264 million in the next four years (3).

With the launch of Venice Declaration of 1980 in which the EC-9 expressed their support for Palestinian self-determination, the Community intensified its funding activities for NGO projects, especially in areas such as health, agriculture, and education. In 1986, the European Community, for the first time, granted preferential access for products originating from the occupied territories (Noor 2004, 33). Later, in the first donor conference held in 1993 following the announcement of the Declaration of Principles (Oslo accords), an international donor mechanism called the Ad Hoc Liaison Committee (AHLC) was created to coordinate the financial aid activities to the Palestinians as well as to review donor and aid policies and strategies.

Under the framework of Oslo, the EU member states made the financial and economic dimension an indispensible element of their engagement with the Middle East peace process, and with nearly €1 billion in grants and loans, and a further €500 million in contributions to UNRWA, the EU became the biggest donor of financial and technical aid to the West Bank and Gaza Strip from 1994 to the end of 2002. Again in the same period, bilateral EU Member State assistance reached an amount of €2.5 billion. The EU, regarding the development of Palestinian economy and the improvement of living conditions in the occupied territories as a decisive element for the peace process as well as for the establishment of a democratic and viable Palestinian state, has committed considerable financial aid to projects aiming at improving the Palestinian infrastructure such as road networks, hospitals, airport, harbour and schools. In addition, a great share of EU aid was committed to the creation of democratic Palestinian institutions of self-government with the aim of establishing the basis of an independent State of Palestine with internationally recognised borders, which the member states consider vital not only for the security of Israel but for the stability of the whole region as well (Asseburg 2003, 12-14).

Since the launch of the Barcelona Process in 1995, the Palestinian Authority has been an equal and full partner of the *Euro-Mediterranean Partnership* (EMP), benefiting from its principal financial instrument, MEDA. Under MEDA, the EU offers technical and financial support instruments to assist the economic and social process in the Palestinian Authority.

On 24 February 1997, the EC and the PLO (representing the Palestinian Authority) signed the Interim Association Agreement on Trade and Co-operation the primary objective of which is to establish basic structures for the liberalisation of Palestinian trade, and to create a framework for a closer cooperation between the EU and the PA in various areas. Nevertheless, as a result of closure and curfews within the West Bank and Gaza Strip since the outbreak of the second intifada in 2000, the implementation of several aspects of the Agreement has been extremely difficult.

Due to the economic losses and the destruction of the Palestinian infrastructure caused by the second intifada, the EU shifted the EU committed its assistance in terms of humanitarian aid and support top refugees and emergency projects such as job creation, establishment of communication networks and the reestablishment of the infrastructure. Yet, even during the intifada the EU member states maintained their long-term objective of supporting the creation of an independent and democratic State of Palestine. At the same time, through various programmes in areas such as reform of the judiciary, health management and public finances, the EU continued to provide state- and institution-building support for the Palestinian Authority (Asseburg 12-14)

Palestinian Authority went in the form of direct budget assistance to secure expenditures such as social, educational health and other facilities. At that time, the EU direct budget assistance was absolutely vital for the survival of the Palestinian government institution for the reason that Israel cancelled the regular monthly transfers of revenues from Israel to the PA as a response to the outbreak of the second intifada (Asseburg 2003, 12-14).

After 2001, the European Commission reorganised its budget support programme made the EC assistance to the PA conditional in progress in reform efforts. Thus, the EU member states agreed to attach clear and concrete reform conditions to EC direct budget support obliging the PA to take the tangible measures for the successful implementation of the basic objectives of the reform process. Therefore, through a number of statements on the Middle East, the EU has underlined that the EC budgetary support, to the PA will only be provided if certain conditions are fulfilled in order to achieve sustainable results.

Since 2004, the Commission has been making the largest financial contribution to the Public Financial Management Reform Trust Fund managed by the World Bank, and created with the aim of supporting the Palestinian Authority's Financial Management Reform Programme. Here again, the continuation of payment to PA is conditional upon the success of the reform process.

In 2006, upon the proposal made by the Quartet, the Community developed and established a Temporary International Mechanism (TIM) with the aim of facilitating direct assistance to the Palestinian population. The Community's contribution to TIM, which covers the expenditures such as costs of hospitals, health care centres, public services, energy supply and social allowances to the poor reached €105 million in 2006. In addition, the Community made available €12 million to the office of the President of the PA to support technical assistance and capacity building. Again in the same year, as a response to the deterioration of the socio-economic conditions of the Palestinian people, the EU committed €184 million for refugees, food/food security aid as well as for humanitarian aid. In total, the Community assistance to the Palestinian people during 2006 was €349 million.

Nonetheless, the considerable EU financial support over the past decade to the Palestinian territories has not achieved the intended results because of the Israeli military reoccupation, the extensive damage inflicted on the Palestinian infrastructure, and closure policies imposed by the Israeli forces that block the daily civilian movement of the Palestinians for security reasons. This has led to devastating consequences for the Palestinian economy, causing net drop in per capita GDP, and further increase in unemployment rates in the West Bank and Gaza Strip, making the Palestinian economy more dependent on international assistance. The EU, in spite of being both the main provider of financial aid to PA and the main trading partner for Israel, failed to produce a diplomatic response to the destruction of infrastructural investments by the Israeli forces, and failed to impose any economic sanctions to Israel, which is the direct consequence of the lack of strategic unity among its members (Asseburg 2003, 12-15; Sayigh 2004, 9-11).

## 5.2. EU Support for Palestinian reforms[17]

Through financial assistance and its participation in the Quartet, the EU gives substantial support to the Palestinian state- and institution-building. Since 2000, the EU has attached reform conditions to its budgetary assistance to the Palestinian Territories, which has led to positive results in key reform measures, such as order and accountability in public finances that aim to bring PA financial system closer to international standards. Through EU-PA Action Plan In the institution-building area, the EU promotes reform efforts regarding financial control and audit, trade liberalisation, development control and management, development of the taxation system, private sector development through facilitating administrative practices and reform of revenue administration. Also, in order to enhance the rule of law, the Commission made financial aid and training available for the judiciary programme that seeks to strengthen the judicial institutions and finances the refurbishment of

---

[17] This part is based on the information provided by the DG External Relations of the European Commission. <http://ec.europa.eu/external_relations/gaza/intro/index.htm#2.3>

selected courts. The aim of judicial reforms is to create an independent and transparent judiciary system in the PA.

The EU also provided considerable financial and technical support to the Palestinian elections. In 1996, for instance, the Union was the general coordinator of Palestinian elections. After the establishment of an independent Central Election Commission (CEC) with the European Commission in 2002, the EU set up an observation mission for the presidential elections in January 2005, and for parliamentary elections in January 2006.

Additionally, the EU promotes the Palestinian reform process through its participation in the Quartet which provides a multilateral framework for further negotiations among the four partners in order to solve the fundamental problems that hinder a long-lasting peace settlement. The EU plays an active role in the implementation of the Roadmap objectives by monitoring the process and offering advice on the creation of a formal monitoring mechanism and its operation.

Nevertheless, the outcome of the state- and institution-building reforms in the Palestinian Territories is far from satisfactory, since the PA still lacks legitimate, transparent and democratic institutions, which were determined as the precondition for the establishment of the State of Palestine in the future. The Palestinian political system is described by Asseburg as being:

> "(...) characterized by the prevalence of informal institutional arrangements and clientèlism, by authoritarian government practices and human rights abuses, and by an inflated and inefficient public sector in which funds are misused. It is also characterised by the lack of influence of the elected representatives, transparency and accountability, checks and balances, the rule of law and an effective monopoly of power" (Asseburg 2003, 18-19).

Again, as in the case of Israel, the European Union failed to give a response to the human rights abuses in the Palestinian Territories, and was unsuccessful in applying any economic and diplomatic sanctions against the PA, which again resulted from the lack of consensus among the member states (Dannreuther 2002, 11).

## 6. EU-Israel[18]

As already discussed in previous chapters, due to a number of historical and ideological reasons, some EU member states such as Germany and the Netherlands tend to pursue a more pro-Israeli stance, whereas the Mediterranean countries like Spain, Italy and Portugal, together with France, seem to be more pro-Arab in orientation. In spite of this division, since the launch of its Middle East Policy in the 1970s, the EU has been criticised by the Israeli side for promoting a pro-Palestinian position in order not to endanger its trade links and economic interests with the region. For this reason, Israel, economically and diplomatically backed by the US, has constantly sought to avoid a strong political EU presence in the Middle East (Noor 2004, 44).

The Israeli mistrust of the European peace efforts in the region was further deepened by the release of the EU survey results in November 2003 which showed that the majority of the citizens in all EU member states (nearly 60% in EU-15) consider that Israel poses a threat to world peace. Interestingly in Netherlands, known for its traditional support of Israel, and in Austria, the percentage is over %65 (85).

Nevertheless, the EU is the main trading partner of Israel, and trade between Israel and the EU is conducted on the basis of the Association Agreement signed in Brussels in November 1995 and which took effect from June 2000. This EU-Israeli Association Agreement includes free trade arrangements for industrial goods and concessionary arrangements for trade in agricultural products and fisheries. It also puts primary emphasis on the importance of regional co-operation as well as on regular bilateral and international political dialogue on scientific, technological and cultural areas, which would contribute to both the political stability and economic progress of the region.

The EU-Israeli relations are governed by the bilateral and multilateral dimensions of the Euro-Mediterranean Partnership (EMP) which aims at creating a Euro-Mediterranean region of peace, stability, democracy and security. In

---

[18] This part mostly rests upon facts and figures provided by the DG External Relations of the European Commission <http://ec.europa.eu/external_relations/israel/intro/index.htm>

contrast to other EMP partners, Israel receives no bilateral funding under MEDA because of its high national income. Yet, it takes participation in youth exchange programmes and other cultural activities supported by the MEDA programme.

In the aftermath of the enlargement in 2004, the EU launched the European Neighbourhood Policy in order to promote political, security, economic and cultural cooperation between the 25 member states and the Union's neighbouring countries. Within the framework of the programme, the partner countries jointly decide on Action Plans, agreeing to commit themselves in various fields such as political dialogue and reform; trade; justice and home affairs; energy; transport; environmental issues; research as well as interpersonal contacts. The EU-Israeli Action Plan was concluded by the Commission in December 2004 as with Morocco, Jordan, Tunisia and the Palestinian Authority. The key areas for the enhancement of cooperation and implementation of the Action Plan were political dialogue and cooperation; industry, trade, services and internal market; justice and legal matters, including closer cooperation in counter-terrorism, terrorism financing and non-proliferation of weapons of mass destruction; research, innovation, education and culture; and facilitation of customs procedures; cooperation in energy and transport.

The same year, following the fifth meeting of the EU-Israel Association Council[19] held in Brussels under the chair of the Netherlands Presidency, the EU issued a Declaration, outlining its standpoint in the EU-Israeli relations and the Middle East question. Stressing on the importance of the Quartet Map point of reference for peace negotiations, the EU once more invited both sides to take concrete measures for the implementation of Roadmap objectives:

> "The Palestinian Authority should make every effort to halt terrorist attacks against Israelis, maintain unity and be prepared for a possible Israeli withdrawal from Gaza and part of the northern West Bank. While recognising

---

[19] The EU-Israeli Association Council is one of the two main bodies for the EU-Israeli dialogue, established by the Association Agreement. The Council, held at ministerial level discuss political and economic issues at regular meetings.

Israel's right to protect its citizens from terrorist attacks, the Government of Israel must exercise this right within the boundaries of international law. Israel should exert maximum effort to avoid civilian casualties and take no action that could aggravate the situation of the Palestinian people. In particular, the EU calls on Israel to end the practices of extra-judicial killings and house demolitions, and halt the construction of the barrier inside the occupied Palestinian Territory including in and around East Jerusalem" (4).

In spite of this forceful declaration, the EU was reluctant or powerless to give an explicit diplomatic response to the Israeli demolition of EU-funded infrastructure in the PA as well as to the human rights abuses committed by the Israeli forces in the occupied territories. This became more evident as the member states became divided over the application of diplomatic and economic sanctions against Israel after the adoption of a resolution by the European Parliament in 2002 that called for the suspension of EU-Israeli Association Agreement. The UK government, usually pro-Palestinian, decided to lift the suspension of its arms sales to Israel due to the US pressure. (Müller 2007, 7-16) The EU member states, even as the Government of Israel announced its plan of constructing the security barrier inside the West Bank, the EU member states failed to pursue a joint diplomatic approach, resulting primarily from the diverging views among the EU member states (Sayigh 2004, 11).

## 7.　EU in the Middle East: A civilian power?

After having critically evaluated the historical development of a common European policy towards the Arab-Israeli conflict, the question that remains to be answered is whether the civilian power concept is a relevant approach to the analysis of the different aspects of the EU's past and present status in the Middle East peace process.

The fundamental characteristic of an ideal civilian power, discussed at length in the second chapter, is the *preference for diplomacy and institutionalised dialogue* in international relations. Indeed, since the beginnings of the European Integration in the 1950s, EU has successfully developed a specific form of diplomacy, both in form and essence, as well as an institutionalised dialogue with several states outside its borders (Whitman 2002).

With regard to the Middle East, the EU initiated the Euro-Arab Dialogue at the Copenhagen European Council in 1973 with the objective of fostering the EC-Arab cooperation in a wide range of areas such as industry, agriculture, science, education, technology, financial cooperation, and infrastructure. Likewise, the Euro-Mediterranean Partnership, launched with the Barcelona Declaration of 1995, aimed to reinforce the economic, social and political relations between the EU member states and the countries of the Southern Mediterranean.

In the bilateral framework, the member states made noteworthy steps in their relations with individual Mediterranean partners through Euro-Mediterranean Association Agreements. The EU has also opened negotiations for bilateral Association and Interim Agreements with Israel and the Palestinian Authority which were underpinned by the European Neighbourhood Policy in 2005.

*The promotion of democracy, human rights, peace and development* is the second feature that a civilian power is expected to possess. Indeed, defining the protection of human rights and promotion of democracy as its key foreign policy objectives as well as a significant condition for association agreements, the EU continues to apply several civilian instruments, including cooperation and development assistance programmes, demarches and election observations with the purpose of encouraging democratisation efforts in third countries.

With regard to the Middle East, the EU has kept its long-term objective of supporting the establishment of an independent, viable and democratic Palestinian State, living in peace with Israel as well as its Arab neighbours, and has committed significant financial assistance to the development of the humanitarian and economic conditions of the Palestinian population in the occupied territories.

Through a number of programmes in areas such as reform of the judiciary, health management, trade, private sector and public finances, the EU member states have provided substantial support to state- and institution-building in the Palestinian Authority. In addition, the EU organised an observation mission for the presidential elections in the Palestinian Territories in January 2005, and for parliamentary elections in January 2006.

Nonetheless, in the cases of human rights abuses by both the Israeli forces in the occupied territories and the Palestinians, the member states have so far been reluctant to impose any diplomatic or economic sanctions on either party. This stems mainly from the lack of political unity among the member states. Similarly, the EU failed to raise its voice against both the lack of transparency in Palestinian political institutions and against the failure of the PA to implement the objectives of the EU-financed democratisation process.

The third feature of an ideal civilian power is the preference for *using economic instruments,* such as the promise of aid, the aid itself, the sanction of aid and other means in the pursuit of foreign policy objectives and interests (Smith 2005). Indeed, humanitarian aid has always occupied a central position in the Union's relations with its Mediterranean partners, including the Palestinians. In close cooperation with non-governmental organisations and UN specialised agencies, and through ECHO, the EU has provided essential equipment and food to the victims of the Arab-Israeli conflict in emergency situations along with cash subsidies in the fields of water sanitation, health and protection. Additionally, as already illustrated, the EU is the main donor to the West Bank and Gaza, having committed approximately €350 million to the

Palestinian Authority in 2006 to improve the socio-economic conditions in the PA as well as to foster the Palestinian reform efforts in state- and institution building (Asseburg 2003).

With the outbreak of the second intifada in 2000, and as a response to the violent attacks on civilians by both the Israeli and the Palestinian side, the European Commission regulated its budget support programme, linking it more closely to concrete progress in reform efforts. Several speeches implied that the EU would maintain its financial assistance programmes in the future, provided that the PA undertakes substantial measures for the successful implementation of the reform objective. In this way, the EU used what Smith defines as "positive conditionality", promising trade agreements, aid, and closer dialogue as long as certain political and economic requirements are fulfilled.

*Commitment to multilateral arrangements* is a further feature of an ideal civilian power to which the EU attaches great value in its external activities, particularly in its pursuit of a fair and long-lasting solution to the Arab-Israeli conflict. Indeed, through a number of declarations on the situation in the Middle East, and through several agreements it has signed with the countries in the region, the Union repeatedly expressed its commitment to multilateral arrangements based on diplomatic tools, international cooperation and the rule of law, as well as its opposition to unilateral initiatives undertaken by the conflicting parties. The Union's disagreement with the unilateral disengagement plan of Israel, the inclusion of a multilateral dimension into the framework of the EMP in order to give all partners a seat at the negotiation table, and its participation in the Middle East Quartet are among the major examples given in the literature.

The Union's inclination towards multilateralism and international cooperation reasonably raised the question of the root causes of this kind of foreign policy behaviour. Many, including the member states, argue that the Union's commitment to multilateral arrangements is because of the positive and encouraging experiences of the member states in international institutions such as the United Nations and the European Union, where international law and collective action in international disputes predominate (Archick 2005). For others, including US critic, Robert Kagan, the European preference for multilateralism lies in its military weakness. The opponents of this view, however, re-fer to the Union's participation in the NATO-led war in Kosovo and the US-led war against the Taliban in Afghanistan (Archick 2005, 4). However, more convincing and all-embracing is the argument made by the analysts who con-sider the institutional constraints of the EU and the decision-making mecha-nism in CFSP to be the key reason for the European support for multilateral solutions (Dannreuther 2002; Dembinski 2002).

In short, a detailed assessment of the past and present involvement of the European Union in the MEPP illustrates explicit elements of its civilian power nature. Yet, there remains the question whether the institutional constraints within the EU foreign policy cooperation and the internal decision-making ap-paratus are once more the root causes for this kind of foreign policy conduct.

As analysed in the third chapter, from the launch of its Middle East Policy in the 1970s, the EU has gradually developed its position from, an observer and a participant, to becoming a crucial partner in the peace process, which is undoubtedly consistent with the institutional improvements in the EU foreign policy cooperation (Noor 2004). Yet, despite its generous financial contribu-tions to the efforts in peace settlement, the EU still finds it difficult to increase its political influence in the region. This is due mainly to the diverging eco-nomic and strategic relations of the EU member states with the countries in the Mediterranean as well as because of their historical experiences in the region.

The lack of coherence among the member states is exacerbated by the struc-tural weaknesses within the EU and the decision-making process in the CFSP pillar. The intergovernmental nature of foreign policy-making and the principle unanimity has hindered the EU from giving rapid reactions in crisis situations, particularly during the first and the second intifada. During this time, the EU declarations did not go beyond "condemning", "urging" and "in-viting" and the member states fail to act as collectively and coherently as in Community affairs of the first pillar (Biscop 2007). Therefore, with regard to the EU's role in the Middle East region, the institutional structure and policy-making mechanism within the CFSP are once more responsible for the civil-ian character of the EU, since they prevent the EU from strengthening its political presence in the region, confining its role to the economic aspects of the Middle East peace process.

## 8. Conclusion

The European Union has never been indifferent to the Middle East. The peaceful settlement of the Arab-Israeli conflict that emerged with the establishment of the State of Israel in 1948 has always been a high priority on the agenda of the European Union. Since the first official declarations in the 1970s, the EC/EU has continuously expressed its concern about the geopolitical turbulences in the Middle East, and sought, at the same time, a more prominent political role in international peace initiatives. Yet, despite the Union's generous financial assistance to the peace process, the EU still faces many hindrances in its attempts to increase its political influence, mainly due to the institutional constraints as well as the decision-making mechanism within the CFSP system.

The Union's interest in the stability of its southern Mediterranean neighbourhood and its willingness to become a politically influential partner in the peace process result from a mixture of factors, including history, economic ties, geography and the sizeable Muslim population in member states, as discussed at length in chapter 3. The historical ties of some European powers with the Arab World which were further reinforced during the colonial ages continue to be a decisive factor in the Union's position towards the conflicting parties. Also, considering the establishment of Israel in the Middle East as the root cause for the emergence of the Palestinian problem, the European continent was unable to remain outside the scope of the Arab-Israeli conflict.

In addition, the geographical closeness of the region determines the European position towards the conflict, and makes the promotion of economic progress and democratization in southern Mediterranean region a key objective for the EU. The demographical trends in the EU capitals are also significant in the sense that the still increasing Muslim population in the Community exercises substantial influence on domestic politics. Similarly, the economic and trading ties of the EU member states with the Mediterranean region are still regarded as one of the most important motivations behind the Union's efforts to gain a more active political role in the peace process.

For all the reasons mentioned above, the European Union has always been interested in the stability and security of its southern Mediterranean neighbourhood and has done its utmost to pursue a common and coherent policy towards the Arab-Israeli conflict. Indeed, since the Venice Declaration in 1980, regarded as the most explicit EC policy statement up to that time, the EU member states has reemphasised the Palestinian right for self-determination whilst acknowledging the Israeli right to exist in a peaceful and secure environment.

Hence, the EU has welcomed any international initiative that presents concrete proposals for conflict resolution, and has expressed, at the same time, its readiness to actively participate in the peace process. Within the framework of the EPC, the member states issued a number of declarations in which they explicitly declared the Union's stance on the Arab-Israeli conflict. Also, with the launch of the Euro-Arab Dialogue, a joint initiative with the EC and the countries of the Arab world, the EU established a politically structured dialogue for long-term economic and political cooperation with its south-eastern neighbours. Yet, the Community's involvement in the peace process has been unable to go beyond declarations and its role has mostly been confined to being a "payer".

It was only with the establishment of the CFSP as the second pillar of the European Union and the appointment of the Javier Solana to the post of High Representative that the EU started to gradually increase its credibility as an influential actor in the Middle East peace process. One of the most successful initiatives undertaken by the EU during that period was the EMP through which the EU created political, economic and security partnership with the Mediterranean region. The importance of the EMP lies, in fact, in that it is the only forum in which the Arab countries and Israel can negotiate.

Again with this programme, the EU gave the Palestinian Authority the status of an equal member, and provided noteworthy financial assistance for socio-economic development in the occupied territories. Moreover, in the same period, with the Berlin Declaration of 1999, the member states explicitly expressed their support for a democratic, viable and peaceful Palestinian state. Lastly, with its participation in the Middle East Quartet, the EU played a crucial role in the preparation of the Roadmap document which is the product of intense negotiations between the Quartet representatives. In addition, the Roadmap is a diplomatic achievement for Europe in the sense that the EU has gained the status as a crucial partner for future negotiations.

Regardless of the indisputable success of the Union through the gradual movement from participant to an influential partner, the shared will of member states to exercise real political influence on the conflicting parties failed to materialise and its role has, for the most part, remained in the economic sphere of peace settlement. Even in the Middle East Quartet, the EU is still not recognised as an equal mediator as the US, and the member states still find it difficult to speak with a single voice when a regional dispute emerges, as was the case when Israel declared its plan for a unilateral withdrawal from the occupied territories and Hamas won the Palestinian elections.

The European failure on the political scene of the Middle East peace initiatives stems primarily from the lack of unity among the member states over a number of issues. Indeed, since the launch of the European Middle East Policy in the 1970s, the lack of coherence has constantly prevented the EU from adopting a common position and giving joint responses in case of regional crises. At this point, the Union has failed to act as a single unity and has focussed its efforts mostly on the economic aspects of conflict resolution.

The problems arising from the disunity among the member states have been made even worse by the institutional complexities and the consensual nature of the decision-making system in the CFSP. The principle of unanimity remains the main obstacle to the Union's ability to apply its power resources as a collective response, and the member states rarely succeed in reaching a consensus on how to react over the attacks on civilians as well as human rights abuses by both sides.

As a result of these institutional constraints, the Union has demonstrated an affinity towards an economic rather than a political engagement. Over the years the EU has preferred to use economic instruments, such as trade agreements and financial aid to state- and institution-building programmes. Likewise, multilateral arrangements based on diplomacy and international law still remain the Union's most desirable foreign policy instruments, which make the EU an almost ideal civilian power.

In fact, with its role in the Middle East peace process and the instruments it applies in the pursuit of its objectives, the EU comes closer to the civilian power model, prioritising civilian means and ends. Yet, although the European commitment to multilateralism and its preference for internationally legitimised solutions, as well as its use of economic instruments, have so far made significant contributions to the peace process, it has become obvious that, in general, "the traditional means in the hands of the European Union as a "civilian power" are not effective when dealing with the Middle Eastern crises" (Silvestre 2003, 50).

For all the reasons mentioned above, the future status of the EU in the peace process depends, for the most part, on the successful elimination of the internal constraints within the CFSP field. The EU will then be able to increase its political presence in the region, and gain credibility as an international actor. The resolution of the conflict needs more EU involvement. As illustrated in detail, the European contribution to international peace initiatives is irreplaceable. Without European budgetary support, the economy of Palestinian Authority would immediately collapse, which could lead to destructive consequences for the security of the region.

Likewise, owing to its traditional pro-Arab orientation, the EU has a vital role to play in the implementation of the Roadmap principles particularly in the establishment of the State of Palestine. However, this can only be achieved if the member states can overcome the internal differences within the foreign policy and intensify their efforts in constructing a more coherent and confident approach towards the peace process. The removal of internal hindrances within the CFSP field would also grant the European Union more credibility as a global actor, in both economic and political terms.

# References

Aaron, D., Beauchenese, A., Burwell, F., Nelson, R., Riley, K., and Zimmer, B. (2004) *The Post 9/11 Partnership: Transatlantic Cooperation against Terrorism.* Policy Paper. Washington: Atlantic Council of the US.

Archick, K. (2005) *European Views and Policies Toward the Middle East.* Congressional Research Service (CRS) Federation of American Scientists [Report for Congress] Washington, D.C.: CRS. http://www.isn.ethz.ch/pubs/ph/l ist.cfm?v33=60194 (accessed 21 March 2007).

Arı, T. (2006) *Uluslararası İlişkiler Teorileri: Çatışma, Hegemonya, İşbirliği.* Istanbul: ALFA Basım Yayım Dağıtım Ltd. Şti.

Asseburg, M. (2003) 'From declarations to implementations? The three dimensions of European policy toward the conflict.' In: Ortega, M. (ed) *The European Union and the crisis in the Middle East.* Chaillot Papers, 62. Paris: EU Institute for Security Studies. 11-26.

Attinà, F. (2003) 'The Euro-Mediterranean Partnership Assessed: The Realist and Liberal Views.' In: *European Foreign Affairs Review.* 8 (2). 181-199.

Balbisi, L. and Szigetvári, T. (2001) *Economic breakthrough by the Mediterranean countries in the context of EU enlargement.* Budapest: Institute for World Economics.

Bertam, C., Schild, J., Heisbourg, F. and Boyer, Y. (2002) *A Franco-German Initiative in European Defence.* Berlin: Stiftung Wissenschaft und Politik (SWP).

Bicchi, F. (2002) *The European Origins of Euro-Mediterranean Practices.* [Paper] 040612. Berkeley: Institute of European Studies. June. http://repositories.cdlib.org/ ies/ 040612 (accessed 21 March 2007).

Biscop, S. (2007) *For a 'More Active' EU in the Middle East. Transatlantic Relations of Europe's Engagement with Iran, Lebanon and Israel-Palestine.* Egmont Paper, 13. Brussels: Royal Institute for International Relations. http://www.irri-kiib.be/pape-regm/ep13.pdf (accessed 24 March 2007).

Bretherton C. and Vogler, J. (2006) *The European Union as a Global Actor.* 2. edn. London: Routledge.

Bull, H. (1982) 'Civilian Power Europe: A contradiction in terms?' In: *Journal of Common Market Studies.* 21 (2). 149-164.

Burchill, S. (1996) 'Realism and Neorealism' In: Burchill S. and Linklater A. (eds) *Theories of International Relations.* Basingstoke: St. Martins Press: 67-92.

Burckhardt, C. (2004). *Why is there a public debate about the idea of a 'Civilian Power Europe?* LSE European Institute Working Paper. London: London School of Economics.

Ciment, J. (1997) *Palestine/Israel: The Long Conflict.* New York: Facts on File.

Cooper, R. (2003) *The European Answer to Kagan.* Weltpolitik. [Online article] http://www.weltpolitik.net/ (accessed 21 March 2007).

Dannreuther, R. (2002) *Europe and the Middle East: Towards a Substantive Role in the Peace Process?* Geneva Centre for Security Policy. [Occasional paper] 39. http://www.isn.ethz.ch/ph/list.cfm?v33=60194 (accessed 21 March 2007).

Dehousse, R. (1990) European Political Cooperation: 1 July 1987-31 December 1988. In: *European Journal of International Law.* 1. 378-388.

Dekanozishlivi, M. (2004) *The EU in the South Caucasus: By What Means, to What Ends?* [Occasional Paper] Tbilisi: Georgian Foundation for Strategic and International Studies.

Dembinski, M. (2002) *Kein Abschied vom Leitbild "Zivilmacht". Die Europäische Sicherheits- und Verteidigungspolitik und die Zukunft Europäischer Aussenpolitik.* Frankfurt: Hessische Stiftung für Friedens- und Konfliktforschung.

Dixon, W. (1994) 'Democracy and the Peaceful Settlement of International Conflict.' In: *American Political Science Review.* 88. 14-32.

Duchêne, F. (1973) 'The European Community and the Uncertainties of Interdependence.' In: Kohnstamm, M. and Hager, W. (eds) *A Nation Writ Large? Foreign Policy Problems before the European Community.* London: Macmillan. 1-21.

Elias, N. (1976) *Über den Prozess der Zivilisation: Soziogenetische und psychogenetische Untersuchungen.* 2 vols. Frankfurt/Main: Suhrkamp.

European Community (1998) 'Document on the European Identity published by the Nine Foreign Ministers.' In: *European Political Cooperation.* 5th ed. Bonn: Press and Information Service of the Federal Republic of Germany. 48-54.

European Community (1998) 'Statement of the Foreign Minister of Belgium to the European Parliament.' In: *European Political Cooperation.* 5th ed. Bonn: Press and Information Service of the Federal Republic of Germany. 152-153.

European Community (1982) *European Political Cooperation.* 4th ed. Bonn: Press and Information Office of the Federal Republic of Germany.

European Community. European Council (1977) *Conclusions of the Sessions of the London European Council.* http://www.weltpolitik.net (accessed 21 March 2007).

European Community. European Council (1980) *Venice Declaration on the Middle East.* House of Representatives of the State of Israel. http://www.knesset.gov.il/process/docs/venice_eng.htm (21 March 2007).

European Union. European Commission (2007) *Annual Review 2006.* Brussels: Directorate General for Humanitarian Aid. 1681-1402.

European Union. European Commission. DG External Relations (2004). *Statement of the European Union*. Fifth Meeting of the Association Council EU-Israel. http://ec.europa.eu/external_relations/israel/intro/eu_decl_121204.pdf (accessed 23 March 2007).

European Union. European Commission. DG External Relations. *The Euro-Mediterranean Partnership*. http://ec.europa.eu/external_relations/euromed/index.htm (accessed 21 March 2007).

European Union. European Commission. DG External Relations. *The EU's Relations with Israel*. http://ec.europa.eu/external_relations/israel/intro/index.htm (accessed 23 March 2007).

European Union. European Commission. DG External Relations. *The EU's Relations with the West Bank and Gaza Strip*. http://ec.europa.eu/external_ relations/gaza/intro/ index.htm#2.3 (accessed 23 March 2007).

European Union. European Commission (2001) *EU-15 and the 12 Mediterranean Partners: Solid Trade Links*. In: Statistics in Focus Theme 6-7, Brussels: Eurostat.

European Union. European Commission. *European Community Humanitarian Aid Department*. http://ec.europa.eu/echo/field/index_en.htm. (accessed 21 April 2007).

European Union. European Commission. *Lomé Covention*. http://ec.europa.eu/development/geographical/cotonou/lomegen/lomeitoiv_en.cfm.

European Union. European Commission (2005) Euromed Information Notes: Euro-Mediterranean Partnership and MEDA Regional Activities. Brussels: EuropeAid Cooperation Office DG.

European Union. European Commission (2004) *European Neighbourhood Policy Strategy Paper*. Communication from the Commission. COM (2004) 373. Brussels: European Commission. http://ec.europa.eu/world/enp/pdf/strategy/strategy_paper_en.pdf (accessed 21 March 2007).

European Union. European Commission (2003) *Iraq and Peace in the World*. Flash Eurobarometer Report 151. Wavre: Taylor Nelson/EOS Gallup Europe. http://ec.europa.eu/public_opinion/ flash/fl151_iraq_full_report.pdf. (accessed 23 March 2007).

European Union. European Commission (2001) *Report on the implementation of the European Initiative for Democracy and Human Rights in 2000*. Commission Staff Working Document SEC (2001) 801. Brussels: European Commission.

European Union. European Commission. *Euro-Mediterranean Interim Association Agreement on Trade and Cooperation*. http://eur-lex.europa.eu/LexUriServ/LexUriServ.do?uri=CELEX:21997A0716(01):EN:HTML (20 November 2010).

European Union. European Commission (1995) *The Euro-Mediterranean Partnership – Barcelona Declaration*. Brussels: European Commission http://ec.europa.eu/externalrelations/euromed/bd.htm (accessed 21 March 2007).

European Union. European Council (1994) *Adoption of the WTO Agreements*. Council Decision. 94/800/EC. Official Journal of the EU. L 336/23. http://europa.eu/scadplus/leg /en/lvb/r11010.htm (accessed 22 March 2007).

European Union. European Council (1999) *Presidency Conclusions: Berlin European Council*. Brussels: Press Office of the Council of the European Union. http://europa.eu/european_council/conclusions/ index_en.htm (accessed 22 March 2007).

European Union. European Council (2000) *Common Strategy on the Mediterranean Region*. Official Journal of the EU. L 183/5. http://ec.europa.eu/external_relations/euromed/common_strategy_med_en.pdf (accessed 23 March 2007).

European Union. European Council (2003) *A Secure Europe in a better World. The European Security Strategy*. Adopted on 12 December 2003 by the European Council in Brussels. http://consilium.europa.eu/uedocs/ cmsUpload/78367.pdf (accessed 23 March 2007).

European Union. European Council (2002) *Presidency Conclusions: Barcelona European Council*. SN 100/1/02, Brussels: Press Office of the Council of the Euroepan Union. http://europa.eu/european_council/conclusions/index_en.htm (accessed 23 March 2007).

European Union. European Council (2001) *Presidency Conclusions: Brussels Extraordinary European Council Meeting*. SN 140/01. Brussels: Press Office of the Council of the European Union. http://europa.eu/european_council/conclusions/ index_en.htm (accessed 23 March 2007).

European Union. European Council (2001) *Presidency Conclusions: Göteborg European Council*. SN 200/1/01. Brussels: Press Office of the Council of the European Union. http://europa.eu/european_council/conclusions/index_en.htm (accessed 23 March 2007).

European Union. European Council (2000) *Presidency Conclusions: Nice European Council*. SN 400/00. Brussels: Press Office of the Council of the European Union. http://europa.eu/european_council/ conclusions/index_en.htm (accessed 23 March 2007).

European Union. European Council (2001) *Presidency Conclusions: Stockholm European Council*. SN 100/01. Brussels: Press Office of the Council of the European Union. http://europa.eu/european_council/conclusions/index_en.htm (accessed 23 March 2007).

European Union. European Council (2002) *Presidency Conclusions: Seville European Council*. SN 200/02. Brussels: Press Office of the Council of the European

Union. http://europa.eu/european_council/ conclusions/index_en.htm (accessed 23 March 2007).

European Union. European Council (1997) *The Amsterdam Treaty.* Official Journal of the EU. C 340. http://europa.eu.int/eur-lex/en/treaties/dat/amsterdam.html (accessed 20 March 2007).

European Union. European Council (1987) *The Single European Act.* Official Journal of the EU. L 169. http://europa.eu/scadplus/treaties/singleact_en.htm (accessed 20 March 2007).

European Union. European Council (2004) *Treaty establishing a constitution for Europe.* Official Journal of the EU. C 310. http://www.unizar.es/euroconstitucion/ Treaties/Treaty_Const.htm (accessed 19 March 2007).

European Union. European Council (2007) *Treaty of Lisbon.* Official Journal of the EU CIG 14/07. http://www.consilium.europa.eu/uedocs/cmsUpload/cg00014.en07. pdf (accessed 20 November 2010).

European Union. European Council (2001) *Treaty of Nice.* Official Journal of the EU. C 80. http://europa.eu.int/eur-lex/lex/en/treaties/index.htm (accessed 21 March 2001).

European Union. European Council (1992) *Treaty on European Union.* Official Journal of the EU. 92/C 191/01. http://europa.eu.int/eur-lex/lex/en/treaties/treaties_ founding.htm (accessed 19 March 2007).

European Union. European Parliament and European Council (2006) *Regulation (EC) No 1889/2006 of the European Parliament and of the Council of 20 December 2006 on establishing a financing instrument for the promotion of democracy and human rights worldwide.* Official Journal of the EU L 386. http://eur-lex.europa.eu/LexUriServ/LexUriServ.do?uri=CELEX:32006R1889:EN:NOT     (accessed 20 November 2010).

European Union. European Parliament. *Communication from the Commission to the Council and the European Parliament - The European Union and the United Nations: the choice of multilateralism* . COM/2003/0526. http://eur-lex.europa.eu/ LexUriServ/LexUriServ.do?uri=CELEX:52003DC0526:EN:HTML (accessed 20 November 2010).

Everts, S. (2003) 'Israel and Palestine: how to promote a negotiated settlement.' In: *The EU and the Middle East: A call for Action.* London: Centre for European Forum. 17-35.

Farnham, B. (2003) 'The Theory of Democratic Peace and Threat Perception.' In: *International Studies Quarterly.* 47. 395-415.

Foradori, P. (2006) *European citizens in arms: the EU's international identity and the militarization of a "civilian power.* Jean Monnet Working Papers BBL 3/2006. University of Trento.

Gardner, B. and Stefanova, R. (2001) *The New Transatlantic Agenda: Facing the Challenges of Global Governance.* Aldershot: Ashgate.

Gerrick, R. (2004) 'The Cotonou Agreement: Will it successfully improve the Small Island Economies of the Caribbean?' In: *Boston College International & Comparative Law Review.* 27 (1). 131-146.

Greilsammer, I. and Weiler, J. (1984) 'European Political Cooperation and the Palestinian-Israeli conflict: an Israeli perspective.' In: Allen, D. and Pijpers, A. (eds) *European Foreign Policy-Making and the Arab-Israeli Conflict.* The Hague: Martinius Nijhoff Publishers. 121-160.

Harpaz, G. (2005) *A Proposed Model for Enhanced EU-Israeli Relations: Prevailing Legal Arrangements and Prospective Juridical Challenges.* Israeli Association for the Study of European Integration (IASEU) at Bar-Ilan University [Working Paper] 4/05. Ramat-Gan: IASEU. http://www.biu.ac.il/SOC/iasei/documents/IASEI-WP3-05-Harpaz.pdf. (accessed 21 March 2007).

Hill, C. (1993) 'The Capabilities-Expectations Gap, or Conceptualizing Europe's International Role.' In: *Journal of Common Market Studies.* 31 (3). 305-328.

Hollis, R. (1997) 'Europe and the Middle East: Power by Stealth?' *International Affairs.* 73 (1). 15-29.

Hubel, H. (1992) 'Germany and the Middle East Conflict.' In: Chubin, S. (ed) *Germany and the Middle East: Patterns and Prospects.* London: Pinter.

Jünemann, A. and Schörning, N. (2002) *Die Sicherheits- und Verteidigungspolitik der "Zivilmacht Europa", Ein Widerspruch in sich?* Report. Frankfurt: Hessische Stiftung für Friedens- und Konfliktforschung.

Kagan, R. (2002) 'Power and Weakness.' In: *Policy Review.* 113. 1-21.

Kaye, D. (2003) 'Bound to Cooperate? Transatlantic Policy in the Middle East.' In: *The Washington Quarterly.* 21 (1). 179-195.

Kirste, K. and Maull, H. (1996) 'Zivilmacht and Rollentheorie.' In: *Zeitschrift für Internationale Beziehungen* 3 (2). 283-312.

Knapp, A. and Wright V. (2006) *The Government and Politics of France.* 5th ed. London: Routledge.

Kříž, Z. (2006) 'German Involvement in the War against International Terrorism. The End of Civilian Power?' In: *Central European Political Studies Review.* 8 (2-3). 122-135.

Leeuwen, M. (1999) *EU and US – security relations and the New Transatlatic Agenda: Two case studies.* Hague: Netherlands Institute of International Relations 'Clingendael.'

Loewen, H. (2006) 'Ostasien und Europa – Partner einer internationalen Ordnungs-politik?' In: *German Institute of Global and Area Studies (GIGA) Focus Asien.* 9. http:// www.giga-hamburg.de/content/publikationen/pdf/gf_asien_0609.pdf (accessed 19 March 2007).

Manners, I. (2002) 'Normative Power Europe: A Contradiction in Terms?' In: *Journal of Common Market Studies.* 40 (2). 235-258.

Manners I. (2006) 'The European Union as a Normative Power: A Response to Thomas Diez' In: *Millennium – Journal of International Studies.* 35 (1). 167- 180.

Marchetti, A. (2005) *Ten Years Euro-Mediterranean Partnership: Defining European Interests for the Next Decade.* Bonn: Centre for European Integration Studies.

Maull, H. (1990) 'Germany and Japan: The New Civilian Powers.' In: *Foreign Affairs.* 69 (5). 91-106.

Maull, H. (1999) *Germany and the Use of Force: Still a Civilian Power?* Trier Working Papers on International Politics 2. Trier: University of Trier.

Maull, H., Frenkler, U., Harnish, S., Kirste, K. and Wallraf, W. (1997) *DFG-Projekt „Zivilmächte": Schlußbericht und Ergebnisse. Deutsche, amerikanische und japanische Außenpolitikstrategien 1985-1995: Eine vergleichende Untersuchung zu Zivilisierungsprozessen in der Triade.* Trier: University of Trier. http://www.politik.uni-trier.de/forschung/workshop/dfgfinal.pdf (accessed 24 April 2007).

Migdalovitz, C. (2006) *The Middle East Peace Talks.* Congressional Research Service (CRS) Federation of American Scientists [Issue Brief for Congress] Washington, D.C.: CSR. http://www.fas.org/sgp/crs/mideast/ IB91137.pdf (accessed 21 March 2007).

Miller R. and Mishrif, A. (2005) 'The Barcelona Process and Euro-Arab economic relations, 1995-2005.' In: *Middle East Review of International Affairs.* 9 (2). 94-108.

Missiroli, A. (2001) 'Introduction.' In: Missorili, A. (ed.) *Coherence for European Security Policy: Debates- Cases- Assessments.* EU-Institute for Security Studies (ISS) Occasional Paper 27. Paris: European Union Institute for Security Studies. 1-17.

Morgenthau, H.J. (1976) *Politics among nations.* 5th edn. New York: Alfred A. Knopf.

Moschella, M. (2004) 'European Union's regional approach towards its neighbours: The European Neighbourhood Policy vis-à-vis Euro Mediterranean Partnership.' In: Attinà, F. and Rossi, R. (eds) *European Neighbourhood Policy: Political, Economic and Social Issues.* Catania: The Jean Monnet Centre of the University of Catania. 58-66.

Mutimer, D. (1990) *Institutional Change and the New European Politics: The European Community, European Political Cooperation and the Western European Union.* York Centre for International and Strategic Studies (CISS) [Occassional Paper]

12. Toronto: CISS. http://www.yorku.ca/yciss/publications/OP12-Mutimer.pdf (accessed 20 March 2007).

Müller, P. (2006) *Europe's political role in the Israeli-Palestinian Peace Process – a comparison of the foreign policies of the "Big-Three" EU Member States vis-à-vis the Peace Process.* Paper presented at BISA Conference at the University of Cork. Cork: University of Cork. http://www.bisa.ac.uk/2006/pps/mueller.pdf (accessed 23 March 2007).

Navon. E. (2006) *Soft Powerlessness: Arab Propaganda and the Erosion of Israel's International Standing.* Paper presented at Herzliya Conference. Herzliya: Institute for Policy and Strategy/Lauder School of Government http://www.herzliya-conference.org/_Uploads/2114Paperlastversion1.pdf (accessed 21 March 2007).

Nonneman, G. (2003) 'A European view of the US role in the Israeli-Palestinian conflict.' In: Ortega, M. (ed) *The European Union and the crisis in the Middle East.* Chaillot Papers, 62. Paris: EU Institute for Security Studies. 33-46.

Noor, S. (2004) 'European Union and the Middle East: A Historical Analysis.' In: *Pakistan Horizon.* 57 (1). 23-46.

Nye, J. (1990) *Bound to Lead: The Changing Nature of American Power.* New York: Basic Books.

Nye, J. (2004) *Soft Power: The Means to Success in World Politics.* New York: PublicAffairs.

Orbie, J. (2006) 'Civilian Power Europe: Review of the Original and Current Debates.' In: *Cooperation and Conflict.* 41 (1). 123-128.

Ottolenghi, E. (2006) *Europe and the Middle East.* BESA Colloquia on Strategy and Diplomacy. Bar-Ilan: BESA Centre for Strategic Studies at Bar-Ilan University. http://www.biu.ac.il/Besa/coll19.pdf (accessed 21 March 2007).

Patten, C. (2000) *The European Union's external policy and the Mediterranean: the case for Israel.* Speech 00/134. http://ec.europa.eu/external_relations/news/patten/speech_00_134.htm. (22 March 2007).

Patten, C. (2001) *Statement on Situation in the Middle East.* Speech 01/222. http://ec.europa.eu/external_relations/news/patten/speech01_222.htm (accessed 23 March 2007).

Peters, J. (2004) *Practices and their Failures: Arab-Israeli Relations and the Barcelona Process.* Institute of European Studies [Paper] 040402. Berkeley: Institute of European Studies. http://repositories.cdlib.org/ies/040402 (accessed 21 March 2007).

Peterson, J. and Bomberg, E. (1999) *Decision-Making in the European Union.* Basingstoke: Palgrave Macmillan.

Posen, B. (2004) 'ESDP and the Structure of World Power.' In: *The International Spectator.* 39 (1). 5-17.

Renk, S. *A critical assessment of EU's policy toward the Middle East peace process and the Palestinian Authority.* Available at: http://www. amcipsreports.net/PDF_books/BookIII13.pdf. (accessed 25 December 2010).

Rosencrance, R. (1998) 'The European Union: A new type of international actor.' In: Zielonka, J. (ed) *Paradoxes of European Foreign Policy.* London: Kluwer Law International. 15-23.

Said, E. (1980) *The Question of Palestine.* London & Henley: Routledge & Keagan Paul.

Sayigh, Y. (2004) 'A Sisyphean Task. Putting the Israeli-Palestinian Peace Process Back on Track.' In: *Istituto Affari Internazionali (ITI) Quaderni.* 6. 7-20.

Schorlemer, S. (2000) 'Menschenrechte und 'humanitäre Interventionen.' In: *Internationale Politik.* 55 (2). 41-48.

Senghaas, D. (1994) *Wohin driftet die Welt? Über die Zukunft friedlicher Koexistenz.* Frankfurt/Main: Suhrkamp.

Silvestri, S. (2003) 'A European view of the US role in the Israeli-Palestinian conflict.' In: Ortega, M. (ed) *The European Union and the crisis in the Middle East.* Chaillot Papers, 62. Paris: EU Institute for Security Studies. 47-51.

Sjursen, H. (2004) 'Security and Defence' In: Carlsnaes, W., Sjursen H., and White, B. (eds) *Contemporary European Foreign Policy.* London: Sage Publications. 59-74.

Smith, H. (2002) *European Union Foreign Policy: What it is and What is Does.* London: Pluto Press.

Smith, K. (2000) 'The End of Civilian Power EU: a Welcome Demise or Cause for Concern?' In: *International Spectator.* 35 (2). 11-28.

Smith, K. (2003) 'European Union foreign policy in a changing world'. Oxford: Blackwell Publishing Ltd.

Smith, K. (2005) *Still 'civilian power Europe'?* Working Paper, 1. London: European Foreign Policy Unit / London School of Economics.

Solana, J. (2002) *Europe's Place in the World.* Speech 0101/02. http://ue.eu.int/ueDocs/cms_Data/docs/pressdata/EN/discours/70719.pdf. (accessed 23 March 2007).

Spyer, J. (2004) 'An analytical and historical overview of British policy towards Israel.' In: *Middle East Review of International Affairs.* 8 (2). 80-102.

Stavridis, S. (2001) *Why the 'Militarising' of the European Union is strengthening the concept of a 'civilian power Europe.* European University Institute (EUI) Working Papers, 17. Florence: EUI Robert Schumann Centre for Advanced Studies.

Stuart, D. T. (1994) *Can Europe Survive Maastricht?* Carlise: Strategic Studies Institute at the US Army War College. http://www.strategicstudiesinstitute.army.mil/pdffiles/ PUB177.pdf (accessed 21 March 2007).

Süer B. and Atmaca, A. (2006) *Arap-İsrail Uyuşmazlığı.* Ankara: Orta Doğu Teknik Üniversitesi (ODTÜ) Publishing House.

Tanner, F. (2002) *North Africa: Exceptionalism and Neglect.* [Occasional Paper] 38. Geneva: Geneva Centre for Security Policy (GCSP). http://www.isn.ethz.ch/pubs/ph/details.cfm?lng=en&id=10673 (accessed 19 March 2007).

Taşpınar, Ö. (2003) 'Europe's Muslim Street.' In: *Foreign Policy.* March/April. 76-77

*The Report of the Sharm-el Sheik Fact-Finding Committee* (2001) [Online] http://www.weltpolitik.net/texte/policy/israel/sheikh.pdf (accessed 22 March 2007).

United Nations. *Security Council Resolutions.* http://www.un.org/documents/ scres.htm (accessed 23 April 2004).

United Nations (1949) *Geneva Convention relative to the Protection of Civilian Persons in Time of War.* http://www.unhchr.ch/ html/menu3/b/92.htm (accessed 24 March 2007).

United Nations. United Nations Relief and Works Agency for Palestine Refugees in the Middle East (2007) *The European Commission and the UNRWA: Improving the lives of the Palestinians.* http://www.un.org/unrwa/publications/pubs07.html (accessed 23 March 2007).

United States. Department of State (2003) *Elements of a Performance-Based Roadmap to a Permanent Two-State Solution to the Israeli-Palestinian Conflict.* http://www.state.gov/r/pa/prs/ps/2003/20062.htm (accessed 21 March 2007).

Wagner, W. and Hellmann, W. (2003) 'Zivile Weltmacht? Die Außen- und Sicherheits- und Verteidigungspolitik der Europäischen Union.' In: Jachtenfuchs, M. and Kohler-Koch, B. (eds.) *Europäische Integration.* 2nd edn. Opladen: Leske + Budrich. 569-596.

Whitman, R. (1998) *From Civilian Power to Superpower?* New York: St. Martin's Press,

Whitman, R. (2002) *The Fall, and Rise, of Civilian Power Europe?* [Paper] 16. Canberra: National Europe Centre at the Australian National University. http://www.anu.edu.au/NEC/ Archive/whitman.pdf (accessed 19 March 2007).

Wolf, S. (2003) *EU Aid for ACP Investment.* [Discussion Paper] 192. Hamburg: Hamburg Institute of International Economics (HWWA). http://opus.zbw-kiel.de/volltexte/2003/596/ (accessed 19 March 2007).

Wolfers, A. (1962) *Discord and Collaboration: Essays on International Politics.* Baltimore: Johns Hopkins University Press.

World Bank (2003) *Two Years of Intifada: Closures and the Palestinian Economic Crisis. An Assessment.* Washington: World Bank.

*Worldviews 2002: European Public Opinion and Foreign Policy.* 2002. Public Opinion Survey conducted by Chicago Council on Foreign Relations (CCFR) and the German Fund of the United States (GMF). http://www.worldviews.org/detailreports/europeanreport.pdf (accessed 20 March 2007).

Youngs, R. (2001) *The European Union and the Promotion of Democracy: Europe's Mediterranean and Asian Policies.* New York: Oxford University Press.

Youngs, T. and Taylor, C. (2007) *The Crisis in Lebanon.* [Online Research Paper] 7/8. London: International Affairs & Defence Section of House of Commons Library. http://www.parliament.uk/commons/lib/research/rp2007/rp07-008.pdf (accessed 19 April 2007).

Youngs, T. (2001a) *Developments in the Middle East Peace Process 1991-2000.* [Research Paper] 1/8. London: International Affairs & Defence Section of House of Commons Library. http://www.parliament.uk/commons/lib/research/rp2001/rp01-008.pdf (accessed 22 March 2007).

Youngs, T. (2001b) *The Middle East Crisis: Camp David, the 'Al-Aqsa Intifada' and the Prospects for the Peace Process.* [Research Paper] 1/9. London: International Affairs & Defence Section of House of Commons Library. http://www.parliament.uk/commons/ lib/research/rp2001/rp01-009.pdf (accessed 22 March 2007).

## Annex I: List of Abbreviations

| | |
|---|---|
| ACP | African, Caribbean and Pacific |
| ASEAN | Association of South East Asian Nations |
| CFSP | Common Foreign and Security Policy |
| COREPER | Committee of Permanent Representatives |
| EAD | Euro-Arab Dialogue |
| EC | European Community |
| ECHO | European Community Humanitarian Aid Department |
| EDC | European Defence Community |
| EIDHR | European Initiative for Democracy and Human Rights |
| EMP | Euro-Mediterranean Partnership |
| ENP | European Neighbourhood Policy |
| EPC | European Political Cooperation |
| ESDP | European Security and Defence Policy |
| EU | European Union |
| GMP | Global Mediterranean Policy |
| MEPP | Middle East Peace Process |
| NATO | North Atlantic Treaty Organization |
| QMV | Qualified Majority Voting |
| PA | Palestinian Authority |
| PLO | Palestinian Liberation Organisation |
| PNC | Palestinian National Council |
| PPEWU | Policy Planning and Early Warning Unit |
| REDWG | Regional Economic Development Working Group |
| PSC | Political and Security Committee |
| SEA | Single European Act |
| UN | United Nations |

## Annex II: United States Security Resolutions

**United Nations Security Council Resolution 242 (November 22, 1967)**

The Security Council,

Expressing its continuing concern with the grave situation in the Middle East,

Emphasizing the inadmissibility of the acquisition of territory by war and the need to work for a just and lasting peace in which every State in the area can live in security,

Emphasizing further that all Member States in their acceptance of the Charter of the United Nations have undertaken a commitment to act in accordance with Article 2 of the Charter.

1. Affirms that the fulfillment of Charter principles requires the establishment of a just and lasting peace in the Middle East which should include the application of both the following principles:

(i) Withdrawal of Israeli armed forces from territories occupied in the recent conflict;

(ii) Termination of all claims or states of belligerency and respect for and acknowledgement of the sovereignty, territorial integrity and political independence of every State in the area and their right to live in peace within secure and recognized boundaries free from threats or acts of force;

2. Affirms further the necessity:

(a) For guaranteeing freedom of navigation through international waterways in the area;

(b) For achieving a just settlement of the refugee problem;

(c) For guaranteeing the territorial inviolability and political independence of every State in the area, through measures including the establishment of de-militarized zones;

3. Requests the Secretary-General to designate a Special Representative to proceed to the Middle East to establish and maintain contacts with the States concerned in order to promote agreement and assist efforts to achieve a peaceful and accepted settlement in accordance with the provisions and prin-ciples in this resolution;

4. Requests the Secretary-General to report to the Security Council on the progress of the efforts of the Special Representative as soon as possible.

**UN Security Council Resolution 338 (22 October 1973)**

The Security Council

1. Calls upon all parties to the present fighting to cease all firing and termi-nate all military activity immediately, no later than 12 hours after the moment of the adoption of this decision, in the positions they now occupy;

2. Calls upon the parties concerned to start immediately after the cease-fire the implementation of Security Council resolution 242 (1967) in all of its parts;

3. Decides that, immediately and concurrently with the cease-fire, negotia-tions shall start between the parties concerned under appropriate auspices aimed at establishing a just and durable peace in the Middle East.

**UN Security Council Resolution 1397 (12 March 2002)**

The Security Council

Recalling all its previous relevant resolutions, in particular resolutions 242 (1967) and 338 (1973),

Affirming a vision of a region where two States, Israel and Palestine, live side-by-side within secure and recognized borders,

Expressing its grave concern at the continuation of the tragic and violent events that have taken place since September 2000, especially the recent attacks and the increased number of casualities,

Stressing the need for all concerned to ensure the safety of civilians,

Stressing also the need to respect the universally accepted norms of international humanitarian law,

Welcoming and encouraging the diplomatic efforts of special envoys from the United States of America, the Russian Federation, the European Union and the United Nations Special Coordinator and others, to bring about a comprehensive, just and lasting peace in the Middle East.

Welcoming the contribution of Saudi Crown Prince Abdullah,

Demands immediate cessation of all acts of violence, including all acts of terror, provocation, incitement and destruction;

Calls upon the Israeli and Palestinian sides and their leaders to cooperate in the implementation of the Tenet work plan and Mitchell Report recommendations with the aim of resuming negotiations on a political settlement;

Expresses support for the efforts of the Secretary-General and others to assist the parties to halt the violence and to resume the peace process.

Decides to remain seized of the matter.

AN INTERDISCIPLINARY SERIES
OF THE CENTRE FOR INTERCULTURAL AND EUROPEAN STUDIES

INTERDISZIPLINÄRE SCHRIFTENREIHE
DES CENTRUMS FÜR INTERKULTURELLE UND EUROPÄISCHE STUDIEN

CINTEUS · Fulda University of Applied Sciences · Hochschule Fulda

ISSN 1865-2255

1   *Julia Neumeyer*
    Malta and the European Union
    A small island state and its way into a powerful community
    ISBN 978-3-89821-814-6

2   *Beste İşleyen*
    The European Union in the Middle East Peace Process
    A Civilian Power?
    ISBN 978-3-89821-896-2

3   *Pia Tamke*
    Die Europäisierung des deutschen Apothekenrechts
    Europarechtliche Notwendigkeit und nationalrechtliche Vertretbarkeit einer
    Liberalisierung
    ISBN 978-3-89821-964-8

4   *Stamatia Devetzi und Hans-Wolfgang Platzer (Hrsg.)*
    Offene Methode der Koordinierung und Europäisches Sozialmodell
    Interdisziplinäre Perspektiven
    ISBN 978-3-89821-994-5

5   *Andrea Rudolf*
    Biokraftstoffpolitik und Ernährungssicherheit
    Die Auswirkungen der EU-Politik auf die Nahrungsmittelproduktion am
    Beispiel Brasilien
    ISBN 978-3-8382-0099-6

6   *Gudrun Hentges / Justyna Staszczak*
    Geduldet, nicht erwünscht
    Auswirkungen der Bleiberechtsregelung auf die Lebenssituation geduldeter
    Flüchtlinge in Deutschland
    ISBN 978-3-8382-0080-4

7    *Barbara Lewandowska-Tomaszczyk / Hanna Puławczewska (Eds. / Hrsg.)*
Intercultural Europe
Arenas of Difference, Communication and Mediation
ISBN 978-3-8382-0198-6

# *Series Subscription*

Please enter my subscription to the *Interdisciplinary Series of the Centre for Intercultural and European Studies*, ISSN 1865-2255, edited by Gudrun Hentges, Volker Hinnenkamp, Anne Honer, Hans-Wolfgang Platzer, as follows:

❐ complete series

starting with
❐ volume # 1
❐ volume # ___
    ❐ please also include the following volumes: #___, ___, ___, ___, ___, ___,

❐ the next volume being published
    ❐ please also include the following volumes: #___, ___, ___, ___, ___, ___,

❐ 1 copy per volume         OR         ❐ ___ copies per volume

## Subscription within Germany:

You will receive every volume at 1$^{st}$ publication at the regular bookseller's price – incl. s & h and VAT.
Payment:
❐ Please bill me for every volume.
❐ Lastschriftverfahren: Ich/wir ermächtige(n) Sie hiermit widerruflich, den Rechnungsbetrag je Band von meinem/unserem folgendem Konto einzuziehen.

Kontoinhaber: _____Kreditinstitut: _____

Kontonummer: _____Bankleitzahl:_____

## International Subscription:

Payment (incl. s & h and VAT) in advance for
❐ 10 volumes/copies (€ 319.80)        ❐ 20 volumes/copies (€ 599.80)
❐ 40 volumes/copies (€ 1,099.80)
Please send my books to:

NAME_____DEPARTMENT_____

ADDRESS _____

POST/ZIP CODE_____COUNTRY _____

TELEPHONE _____EMAIL_____

date/signature_____

Please fax to: **0511 / 262 2201 (+49 511 262 2201)**
or mail to: *ibidem*-Verlag, Julius-Leber-Weg 11, D-30457 Hannover,Germany
or send an e-mail: ibidem@ibidem-verlag.de

*ibidem*-Verlag

Melchiorstr. 15

D-70439 Stuttgart

info@ibidem-verlag.de

www.ibidem-verlag.de
www.ibidem.eu
www.edition-noema.de
www.autorenbetreuung.de